Natural & Organic Liquid Soap Making Business Startup

Learn How to Make Shampoo, Conditioner, Body Wash, Sunscreen Lotion, Muscle Balm, Hand Sanitizers, Pet Shampoo & So Much More

By

Ann Robinson

Published by:
www.Valenciapub.com

Valencia Publishing House
P.O. Box 548
Wilmer, Alabama 36587

Cover & Interior designed

By

Alex Lockridge

First Edition

Table of Contents

Foreword

If you are like me, then I am sure you have been using store bought soaps, shampoos, conditioners and other products like so many of us have been doing for so many years. I still remember it was March of 2004 when I had to go to the doctor for some rash that I developed around my back, neck and some of my arm. At first I thought it was some type of allergy, but after many doctors' visits and allergy tests, my dermatologist narrowed it down to one conclusion that my skin became sensitive to some of the chemical in the commercial soap, shampoo, and conditioners that I was using and advised me to use natural soaps, shampoos, and conditioners.

During those two months of going from doctors to doctors and having various tests done, the rash turned into a bad discoloration of those areas; I cried every night as I didn't want to show my neck or arm to anyone. It was a living nightmare, but I was determined to change it.

I started doing research both on and offline and talking to anyone who knew anything about natural soap. In 2004 internet didn't have as much information as it does now. I started going to various libraries and even went to see a Chemistry professor to learn about various chemicals and their potentially harmful effects.

It was November of 2004 when I did my first trial of making all natural shampoo. It smelled horrible, but I kept using it. Next, I made body wash, then liquid soap followed by conditioners. Everything I made, I made it for my own family, never with the intention to sell them.

As I kept trying to improve my recipes and process, I started to try various ideas, process, and ingredients, and by 2009 I perfected the process. By then, I knew my products could stand up to any store bought natural products and beat them fair and square. But most important thing was that just after a year of using my own soaps and shampoos, my skin began to heal, and the discoloration started to disappear, so I knew I did something right not only for me but for the whole family.

It wasn't until 2012 when my husband got laid off from his job, I had to seriously think about how to turn my passion into a small home based business, and I did. I grew my business into a decent business making not only Shampoos or liquid soaps, but I ventured into making body scrubs, body wash, SPF lotions, muscle rubs, bug repellent, hand scrub(mostly for my husband, so he can use after working on his 65 Mustang), hand sanitizer and even dog shampoo for our 10 years old Dalmatian.

This book is not about my success in business, but I want to focus on you and your ability to make your passion into a home based business which can potentially grow into a big business. Lately the new trend is all organic and all natural, so I think this is the right time to get into this business.

I put my best efforts to make this book easy to read and follow so you can get started and see a big success in a short period of time.

In this book, my goal is to you make you understand and learn how each ingredient works with each other and how to create your own recipes and flavors, so your creative side comes out and create something unique that is truly yours and only yours. If you are looking to learn the process, then this is the book for you but if you are just looking just for recipes then this not the book for you.

Before we get into the actual process of creating liquid soap, let's take a moment to look a little closer at why you should make your own products and all the health benefits of doing it.

PART – 1

How to Make Liquid Soap, Shampoo, Conditioner, Dog Shampoo, Body Wash, Body Scrub, Hand Sanitizers, Muscle Balm and so Much more.

Research Your Products

Before you use any store bought products, you want to research the ingredients you'll be putting on your body. There are five places to go for helpful information:

1. **The Internet -** The internet is full of information, but you need to be careful of your sources. Only trust information that comes from non-biased websites. Still, doing a Google search can be a good place to start your research.

2. **Health Publications -** These articles are very informative for products. Just make sure the publications are quality health publications.

3. **Documentaries -** Like the internet, these can be good sources of information; but you need to consider where they are coming from and their motivation. Go for a well-made documentary and not one with an agenda that you don't agree with.

4. **Health Care Providers -** Ask your doctor for their opinion. They can give you an unbiased and clear opinion. However, you still don't have to agree with everything they say.

5. **Family and Friends -** Talk to anyone whom you think has useful information. Just make sure you know where they are getting their information. If needed you can also challenge their information by checking other sources.

Once you have some solid sources, learn all you can learn about products and/or ingredients. You'll quickly find specific products and ingredients that you are more comfortable with. You'll also find information that surprises you. When considering products and ingredients, be sure to find answers to the following questions:

- ✓ Why do you want in the product?
- ✓ What are the ingredients and what do you already know about them?
- ✓ Are the ingredients truly natural?
- ✓ Where do the product and main ingredients come from?
- ✓ Is the product cost-effective?
- ✓ Do you or your family have allergies or medical conditions that can be affected by the product?
- ✓ Is the company a trusted and/or well-known one?
- ✓ Are you more comfortable with a simpler alternative?
- ✓ Is the product right for you and your family?

The Benefits of Research

It will take time, effort and focus in order to research products. However, you will enjoy many benefits. You will have peace of mind in the ingredients and/or products you choose to use; you will enjoy the potential savings; there can be health benefits, and you'll have knowledge and information you can pass on to others. Now that you know the whys of creating your own products, let's look at what you need to have on hand.

Essential Ingredients

If you are going to make your own body care products at home, there are some specific ingredients you need to have on hand. These items are important to have on hand, and you may want to consider purchasing some items in bulk. Let's consider what you should have on hand. But first, let's go through each item and see how they work, then you can decide which ones you will need and which you won't.

Pure Aloe Vera Gel

This isn't the green variety you find at drug stores. A pure aloe vera gel has no added chemicals. Aloe vera gel is healing, moisturizing and pH-balancing. You can use aloe vera gel in a number of products from shampoo to hand creams.

Apple Cider Vinegar

This is a very useful ingredient for body care products. It helps greatly with itchy, dry skin by restoring natural pH levels of the skin and hair. It also has astringent properties. Consider using it in conditioners and in blemish treatments.

ARROWROOT POWDER

This ingredient is similar to cornstarch, but you don't have to worry about the possibility of genetically modified corn. The absorbent properties of this powder makes it an excellent ingredient in body powders and deodorants.

BAKING SODA

This product can be used in a variety of projects. It can be used for a gentle exfoliating facial scrub, shampoo and even oral care products such as toothpaste and mouthwash. You may want to consider having two baking sodas on hand. The cheaper baking soda can be purchased in bulk for making cleaning products. Natural baking soda doesn't undergo a chemical process and can be used for natural body care products.

Bar Soap

Many don't consider this, but you should have several bars of natural or homemade soap on hand. You can grate these into flakes in order to make dish soap and laundry soap among others.

Beeswax

This comes from honeybee hives. It can be melted down for body care products or as an emulsifier. It is great for lip balms, lotions, and ointments.

Borax (Sodium Borate)

This is important to have on hand in bulk if you want to make your own cleaning products such as laundry detergent and dishwashing liquid. It can also be used as a multi-purpose cleaner known for its whitening, stain-removing, and deodorizing capabilities.

Cosmetic Butters

Some great options for body care products include cocoa butter, shea butter, and mango butter. They provide a creamy texture to natural body care products. They are healing, soothing and moisture-rich.

Liquid Castile Soap

This is a gentle olive oil-based soap that works for a variety of cleaning and body care products. It works great for everything from facial cleanser to windshield washer fluid. It is gentle enough to be used in baby care products but tough enough to clean tile grout.

Citric Acid

This is a weak, organic acid that you can add to homemade cleaning products to reduce and eliminate streaking and cloudiness. For body care products it can work as a natural preservative.

Coconut Oil

This is a must have item for body care and beauty products. It can be used in a variety of creams, hair treatments, and other beauty products. The usefulness of Coconut oil are endless; it can even be used as an after-sun treatment. It features natural antibacterial properties, so it can be very beneficial for your skin.

Distilled White Vinegar

This is an excellent ingredient to have on hand for homemade cleaning products. Most hard surfaces can be cleaned effectively and safely with this ingredient either full strength or diluted. Vinegar is also a natural disinfectant that can cut grease, remove soap residue and remove stains. If you don't want to use harsh chemicals or bleach in your home, then consider using vinegar instead.

Essential Oils

If you aren't going to be making large batches of homemade body care products, you won't need a whole lot of essential oils. At the very least you should have one or two essential oils on hand. The best ones are those with antibacterial, antifungal and antiviral properties.

Adding a few drops of essential oils to homemade body care products will increase the cleaning power. Essential oils are also the way you can customize a body care product to your specific hair/skin type. Essential oils are also the way to add a pleasant scent to your homemade products. Some of the best ones to consider are tea tree, lavender, peppermint or lemon since they offer all three benefits.

3% HYDROGEN PEROXIDE

We all know the goodness of Hydrogen Peroxide when it comes to first aid treatments, but this ingredient is also good for the environment and can also be used in place of harsh chemicals like bleach and ammonia. It works great as a stain remover, cleaner, and disinfectant.

LIGHT, NON-GREASY OILS

Pure oils are an important part of your home ingredient collection. They offer excellent skin conditioning and moisturizing properties. Olive oil is a popular ingredient in many personal care products, but there are a number of other lighter and quickly-absorbed oils you can use as well; such as jojoba, grapeseed or sweet almond. You can use oils in shampoos, soaps, body scrubs, lip balms, hair treatments and even as an undiluted moisturizer for your face.

VEGETABLE GLYCERIN

You can use vegetable glycerin as an emollient. This will attract moisture from the air in order to improve the softness of your skin. Add just a little bit of this to your personal care products to have skin benefits.

VITAMIN E OIL

This ingredient works both as a natural preservative and a skin-nourishing oil in skin care recipes, or it can be added simply as a moisturizing ingredient. It is an ideal ingredient when making products for mature or damaged skin due to its antioxidant properties.

VODKA

This is an ingredient most don't think of, but it can actually be quite useful in your body care products. High-proof or grain alcohol vodka works as a natural preservative to help extend the shelf life of your homemade products. It can also be used as a base for homemade spray deodorant or as a glass cleaner to reduce streaking.

WASHING SODA

This is a great natural laundry booster, but it can also be dissolved in solutions to help cut grease, deodorize or disinfect.

These are just a few of the most common ingredients to have on hand. After you read through some of my recipes and ideas, you might decide to focus on a specific product. Depending on what you focus on, your list of ingredients to have on hand may vary. Now let's take a moment to look a little closer at two of the most important aspects of liquid personal care products: essential oils and carrier oils.

How to Use Essential Oils

When you first start making homemade personal care products, essential oils can be quite intimidating. Essential oils come in a tiny bottle and using the right amount, at the right mix can make all the difference between a great personal care product and a disaster.

If you're having a hard time using essential oils, it is important to remember that they are very versatile and unique plant extracts that should be used at a precise measurement in your personal care products. There are a variety of ways in which you can use essential oils.

What Are Essential Oils?

Essential oils are basically a highly concentrated, pure plant extract. Plant essential oils are extracted in one of two ways: simple pressure extraction or steam distillation. Most citrus oils are obtained through simple pressure extraction while steam distillation is used for most other essential oils.

Due to the concentration of essential oils, they are very volatile. This is why you will only find essential oils in small amounts; only a few drops are needed to make most applications effective. The main benefit of essential oils is the wonderful scent they give your homemade products, but they can also offer a number of healing and therapeutic benefits as well.

Essential oils are extremely fragile and need to be stored properly in order to last for their maximum shelf life. You need to store them in dark bottles, away from sunlight and heat. Under these conditions, essential oils can last for several years. The exception to this is citrus oils, which are only good for six to twelve months. Once essential oils are exposed to heat or light for any period of time they will start to oxidize and degrade, as this continues they will lose their beneficial properties.

In addition to properly storing your essential oils, you also need to handle them carefully. Some essential oils can be irritating to the skin, especially if undiluted. Therefore, you should always keep essential oils out of reach of children and pets. Some essential oils should be avoided when pregnant, as you'll see in the table below:

Essential Oil	Danger
Bitter Almond	Toxic
Aniseed	Anethole Rich
Angelica	Emmenagogue
Basil	Possible Irritant
Birch	Possible Irritant
Black Pepper	Skin Sensitization
Boldo Leaf	Toxic
Buchu	Liver Hazardous
Calamus	Toxic
Camphor	Toxic
Cassia	Skin Sensitization
Cedarwood	Emmenagogue
Chamomile	Emmenagogue
Cinnamon	Emmenagogue and Skin Sensitization
Clary Sage	Emmenagogue

Clove	Skin Sensitization
Elecampane	Skin Sensitization
Fennel	Anethole Rich
Fir	Possible Irritant
Ginger	Emmenagogue
Horseradish	Toxic
Hyssop	Possibly Toxic
Jaborandi Leaf	Toxic
Jasmine	Emmenagogue
Juniper	Emmenagogue
Lemon	Possible Irritant
Lemongrass	Possible Irritant
Marjoram	Emmenagogue
Melissa	Possible Irritant
Mugwort	Toxic
Mustard	Toxic
Myrrh	Emmenagogue
Nightshade	Toxic
Nutmeg	Skin Sensitization
Oregano	Skin Sensitization

Parsley Seed	Apiol Rich
Pennyroyal	Toxic
Peppermint	Emmenagogue
Pine	Skin Sensitization
Rose	Emmenagogue
Rosemary	Emmenagogue
Rue	Toxic
Sage	High Thujone Content
Sassafras	Toxic
Savin	Toxic
Savory	Potentially Toxic
Southernwood	Toxic
Stinging Nettle	Toxic
Tansy	Toxic
Thuja	Toxic
Thyme	Possible Irritant
Wintergreen	Toxic
Wormseed	Toxic
Wormwood	Toxic

9 Everyday Oils
just a quick look

Head ache

Joint pain

Better sleep

Back pain

Colds & flu

Stress

Skin care

Cough & phlegm

Disin fectant

In addition to being cautious around essential oils when pregnant, you also need to carefully plan your essential oil usage if you plan to use the products for children. Consider the following essential oils that are safe to use for children:

✧ Bergamot

✧ Cedarwood

✧ Chamomile

- Cypress
- Frankincense
- Geranium
- Ginger
- Lavender
- Lemon
- Mandarin
- Marjoram
- Tea Tree
- Orange
- Rose
- Rosemary
- Rosewood
- Sandalwood
- Thyme

When using essential oils for children products, you should also follow a few specific safety guidelines. Always halve the strength than what the original recipe calls for when using essential oils for children.

Ways to Use Essential Oils

When it comes to personal care products, there are plenty of good ways you can use essential oils. Let's consider ten of the best ways you can get into using your essential oils.

BATHS

Perhaps the best way to get used to essential oils and their fragrance is to try them in baths first. Add about five to ten drops of essential oils to a full bathtub. Not only can you experiment with the therapeutic effects of essential oils, but you can see how the scents work out, so you have a better idea of using the essential oils in your personal care products. Try a few, but one at a time and make a note of how you like the aroma of each.

POTPOURRI OR ROOM SPRAYS

If you don't want to add toxins to the environment around you, then replace your chemical air fresheners with a homemade aromatherapy room spray. This gives you a chance to experiment with mixing your essential oil scents.

Here is a simple mix ratio for DIY homemade air fresheners

Air Freshener Spray Formula:

- 3/4 cup water (tap or distilled)
- 2 tablespoons vodka or rubbing alcohol
- One of the essential oil combinations from below

For Citrus inspired air fresheners try this

- 5 drops wild orange essential oil
- 5 drops lemon essential oil
- 5 drops lime essential oil
- 5 drops grapefruit essential oil

For Room Deodorizing air Fresheners try this

- 4 drops Tea tree oil
- 8 drops lemon essential oil
- 5 drops eucalyptus oil

The possibilities are truly endless. This is a great way to experiment with various essential oils and create a unique blend of aroma that is uniquely yours.

FOOT SOAKS

This is another easy way to try your hand at working with essential oils. Various essential oils can be added to a foot bath to help with sore, tired feet. For this don't mix a few oils instead try one at a time and see which you like the best.

BODY SCRUB

Body scrubs are an excellent way to exfoliate dry, rough skin so you can have smooth and soft skin in the winter. Adding essential oils to your basic body scrub recipe will help you to add a beautiful therapeutic fragrance.

Home Cleaning

While this isn't a personal care product, it can be a way to improve the environment around you. Most essential oils have some type of antibacterial, anti-fungal or anti-viral properties (as I mentioned earlier). So when you add essential oils to your homemade cleaners, you will be able to improve their cleaning benefits.

Skin Moisturizer

As you gain experience in making personal care products and adding essential oils to them, skin moisturizer is a fun project where you can experiment and eventually create something unique that is truly yours. You can add a number of ingredients together to make various skin moisturizers, and any number of essential oils can be added for a pleasant and therapeutic fragrance.

FACIAL CLEANSER

Essential oils have astringent, anti-inflammatory and anti-bacterial properties that make them excellent for use in facial cleansers. You'll just need to use a little more care when formulating your recipe to avoid any sensitivities around your eyes when using essential oils in a facial cleanser.

BUG REPELLENT

Most don't think of adding essential oils to bug repellent, yet there are plenty of essential oils that can be beneficial in deterring bugs. Some great essential oils for insect repellent include the following:

❖ Citronella

❖ Eucalyptus

❖ Lemongrass

❖ Tea Tree

❖ Peppermint

- ❖ Cypress
- ❖ Rose Geranium
- ❖ Bergamot
- ❖ Lemon

Combine any of these scents to make a natural bug repellent come bug season.

MASSAGE OIL

For an excellent massage oil, you need to light a base oil such as grapeseed or sweet almond. You can then add three to five drops of essential oil in a small puddle of oil in your hand. Or if you need larger amounts on hand or to sell then you can add 40-60 drops per 4 ounces of oil.

ORAL HYGIENE

Another place where you can reduce your use of chemicals in by making your own toothpaste and mouthwash. Just a few drops of essential oils can give you a fresh taste in your mouth while helping to provide valuable therapeutic effects.

You can have fun while experimenting with essential oils as long as you take the necessary precautions. There is a lot of learning when it comes to essential oils, but these ten simple projects can help you get started and become more comfortable working with essential oils. Next, let's consider some basic guides in adding essential oils to shampoos and creams.

Adding Essential Oils to Shampoo

Essential oils are a wonderful addition to shampoo. Not only does it offer an aromatic effect, but depending on the scent you choose it can also offer additional therapeutic benefits. However, you do need to make sure you dilute the essential oils to a suitable level to avoid any eye irritation.

Refer to the table we've already included to avoid essential oils that act as irritants. Perhaps the best addition to shampoo is a rosemary essential oil. If you aren't sure about an essential oil, test it on a small patch of skin to see if you are allergic to it or not. When adding essential oils to shampoo consider the following table to guide you through proper dilutions:

Age	Shampoo Amount	Essential Oil Amount
65+	100 ml	10 drops
12-65	100 ml	20 drops
4-12	100 ml	10 drops
1-4	100 ml	2 drops
Under 1	100 ml	Not Recommended
Pregnant	100 ml	5 drops

Adding Essential Oils to Creams

When you choose to mix essential oils with an unscented cream base, you will be adding not only fragrance but also therapeutic qualities to the cream. This gives you a great, non-oily way of applying essential oils. This is of particular benefit to individuals who have skin conditions that can't tolerate carrier oils (will discuss next). When making an essential oil cream then total percentage of essential oil to cream shouldn't go over 2%. You also need to make sure you aren't mixing any essential oil that causes irritation or that you are allergic to. Once you've made the cream, you should keep it in a closed container in a cool place. Consider the following table when diluting your essential oils in a cream base:

Age	Cream Amount	Essential Oil Amount
65+	50 grams	10 drops
12-65	50 grams	20 drops
4-12	50 grams	10 drops
1-4	50 grams	4 drops
Under 1	50 grams	2 drops
Pregnant	50 grams	4 drops

Essential Oil Safety

For all their benefits, essential oils are still very powerful compounds that need to be handled with care. When you choose to work with essential oils, be sure to follow the safety rules below to avoid any issues:

➢ Never use essential oils internally unless a medical practitioner advises you to.

➢ Keep essential oils out of reach of children and pets.

➢ Always dilute essential oils with a carrier oil before applying to the skin.

➢ Essential oils should only be used with the guidance of a certified individual if you are pregnant, lactating or suffer from epilepsy, hypertension, cancer or liver damage.

➢ Use caution when using essential oils around children.

- ➤ Always do a skin patch test with essential oils before using them extensively.

- ➤ If you notice any irritation with an essential oil or specific formula, then discontinue use immediately.

- ➤ Don't get essential oils in your eyes or on mucous membranes.

- ➤ Always wash your hands after handling undiluted essential oils.

- ➤ Be careful when using essential oils when pregnant since certain oils can affect the urinary system and uterus; leading to contractions and premature delivery.

- ➤ You also want to use care in choosing essential oils when nursing since you don't want to transfer them to the baby.

- ➤ It is best to avoid alcohol while using essential oils.

- ➤ Some essential oils can interfere with prescription medications, so use caution.

➢ If you are using an essential oil known for sun sensitivity then avoid sun exposure.

➢ If you have sensitive skin, always test essential oils before using them.

Carrier Oils

As you probably noticed, I've mentioned something called carrier oils a few times now. If you've been doing homemade projects, you may already know about carrier oils and most of their varieties. There are quite a few types of carrier oils, and each one is best for specific uses such as cooking, herbal remedies, and personal care products. When you start making homemade products, it is best to have a few different types of carrier oils on hand. I'm going to discuss a few different types of carrier oils available, but you should experiment and determine which you prefer working with and then keep them on hand.

ALMOND OIL

Almond oil offers moisturizing properties and is used in a number of projects that require a carrier oil, especially those that require a product to remain liquid at room temperature. It can be used as a base oil or mixed with other carrier oils. However, you should avoid using this oil if anyone has nut allergies.

APRICOT KERNEL OIL

If you can't use almond oil for any reason, then this can be a suitable replacement. This is also a good moisturizing oil that is gentle on the skin, making it great for products used on those with sensitive skin or children. This too can be used as a base oil or mixed with other carrier oils.

Avocado Oil

Avocado oil is the same as the fruit it comes from, it is high in essential fatty acids and fat-soluble vitamins. It is a deeply moisturizing oil that is often used in products for those with sensitive skin or skin problems such as eczema. It is best to use avocado oil along with other carrier oils. However, avocado oil is best avoided by those who have a latex allergy. You should do a small skin test with avocado oil before using it as a carrier oil to make sure there is no reaction.

Castor Oil

Castor oil is similar to coconut oil in the fact that it has antifungal, antibacterial and antiviral properties. It is often used in topical products that offer relief from painful and or irritated skin. It is best used with other carrier oils.

Coconut Oil

This is often the most popular carrier oil since it offers many beneficial properties. It offers all three benefits of antifungal, antibacterial and antiviral. This makes it perfect for ointments or skin care products such as diaper rash cream or lip balm. Coconut oil is also an excellent moisturizer that absorbed quickly into the skin. However, coconut oil is solid at room temperature so if you want a liquid product you are going to need to use it along with another carrier oil.

GRAPESEED OIL

Grapeseed oil can be used for more than a cooking oil; it also makes a great carrier oil. It works best in homemade creams and lotions. It can be used as a base or added to other carrier oils.

JOJOBA OIL

This is another common oil found in a lot of bath and beauty recipes along with herbal remedies. It is an excellent carrier oil for adding essential oils too if you want a massage oil. This oil is one that closely matches the natural oils of your skin and absorbs easily without being greasy. It can be used as a base oil or mixed with other carrier oils.

OLIVE OIL

There are plenty of uses for extra virgin olive oil including cooking, beauty products, herbal remedies, cold-process soap and more. It is also the best carrier oil for herbal infusions for both cooking and medicinal purposes. If you are making a salve, it is best to mix it with a base carrier oil due to its strong scent. When diluted with other carrier oils it does absorb well.

PALM KERNEL OIL

This is an important ingredient in homemade bar soap. In a soap recipe, palm oil can give you a firm bar with a great lather. It can also be added to natural beauty products as a moisturizer. It is best used with other carrier oils. However, there is much debate over using this carrier oil since most sources aren't sustainable and the refining process is known to damage the rain forests. So make sure you choose a palm kernel oil source that is sustainably sourced.

ROSEHIP SEED OIL

This is a great option for mature skin since it is high in antioxidants and is ideal for products that deep heal the skin. If you want a product that works for dry, weathered skin or scars are an issue, then definitely have this carrier oil on hand. It is best used with other carrier oils.

Safety and Storing for Carrier Oils

It is important that you store carrier oils in a cool, dark place in order to increase their shelf life. Always smell the oil before using them, and if they smell off, then this means they are likely rancid and should be discarded. If you haven't used a carrier oil before it is important that you do a small skin test for reactions before applying to a large part of your body.

Now that we know some of the basics of liquid soap and the ingredients let's look at the basic process for making liquid soap.

How to Make Liquid Soap

Whether you've been making home projects like cold and hot process soaps for a while, or you are entirely new to the homemade project idea; learning how to make liquid soap isn't that difficult. It may seem as simple as grating some bar soap and then pouring hot water over it, but there is a lot of specific recipes that go into making various liquid soap options such as shampoos, conditioners, body washes and other similar products. Let's first take a look at a basic liquid soap process and then we'll look at some specific project ideas that use liquid based soap.

Ingredients You Will Need

When it comes to liquid soap, it is very similar to hot and cold process soap in the sense that it has a lye component and an oil component. This biggest difference is in the lye part.

When you make a hard bar soap, you will use sodium hydroxide, while liquid soap uses potassium hydroxide. Potassium hydroxide can be harder to find and comes in flakes rather than beads. While the flakes are easier to work with they are still caustic so you should wear gloves and protective eyewear when working with this ingredient.

For liquid soap, you are also going to need a small amount of borax. Some other ingredients you'll need on hand include water, coconut oil, olive oil, essential oils, and colors. You can get all of these ingredients in natural and organic formats if that is something you are looking for.

Equipment You Will Need

As with the hot process soap making, you are going to need a slow cooker, a stick blender, a quart jar and plastic stirring spoons. Most liquid soap recipes measure in ounces, so it is also a good idea to have a kitchen scale. Some additional equipment you may want to get to make the process easier include a plastic potato masher and a large jar for the resting period. In order to move your soap easier, consider having a thermometer and ladle. Additional water is needed to dilute the soap paste and mix with borax in order to neutralize the soap.

(Image of Borax)

Borax, also known as sodium borate, sodium tetraborate, or disodium tetraborate, is an important boron compound, a mineral, and a salt of boric acid. Powdered borax is white, consisting of soft colorless crystals that dissolve easily in water.

Borax has a wide variety of uses. It is a component of many detergents, cosmetics, and enamel glazes.

Liquid Soap Recipe

Follow this ratio and create your own flavor.

- ➤ 16.5 ounces olive oil or other preferred carrier oil
- ➤ 7 ounces coconut oil or other preferred carrier oil
- ➤ 5.5 ounces potassium hydroxide
- ➤ 16.5 ounces distilled or filtered water
- ➤ 40 ounces distilled or filtered water
- ➤ 3 ounces borax
- ➤ 6 ounces distilled or filtered water
- ➤ Essential oils of your choice
- ➤ Optional color of your choice

The Soap Making Process

1. Weigh olive oil and coconut oil or other carrier oils and place them in the slow cooker on low.

2. In a quart jar, weigh the water. Slowly add the weighed potassium hydroxide and stir gently while adding. Don't worry about any sounds or reactions that occur, these are normal.

3. Once the potassium hydroxide is mixed completely and the solution is clear, add it to the oils. There is no need to worry about the temperature at this point.

4. Stir carefully by hand for five minutes to make sure all the oils come into contact with the water/potassium hydroxide mixture.

5. After five minutes you can start stirring with a stick blender. It can take up to thirty minutes to reach "trace". This is normally when the mixture reaches a thick, vanilla pudding like consistency; but when using potassium hydroxide trace may appear more like applesauce.

6. Even if the mixture looks like it is going to separate, don't stop until you reach trace.

7. Allow to cook in the slow cooker for 30 minutes with the lid on. After 30 minutes check the mixture, if it has separated then stir it back in.

8. Check the mixture every 30 minutes for the next three to four hours.

STAGES TO WATCH FOR

During this three to four-hour cooking stage, you will notice the soap mixture goes through several stages. They will typically appear as the following:

✧ Trace - thick pudding to applesauce appearance.

✧ Custard like appearance with small bubbles.

✧ Watery mashed potatoes appearance.

✧ Taffy appearance and consistency.

✧ Chunky to creamy petroleum jelly appearance.

✧ Translucent petroleum jelly appearance.

Each of these stages will typically take 30 minutes or longer. You'll need to be patient. The first time you'll likely feel like it won't work, but just give it time, and it will eventually come together. You should be able to stir it at each stage except the taffy stage. This is when you may need the potato masher. This step will be the most difficult to stir, but you need to keep going since you are almost finished.

Soap Testing and Finishing Stages

Once you reach the last stage and it appears translucent, you can test your soap. Add about one ounce of soap paste to two ounces of boiling water. Stir until it dissolves. Allow it to sit for a few minutes. If it turns clear or remains slightly cloudy, then your soap is ready. If it turns really cloudy or milky, then you should cook the soap for another 30 minutes or so before testing again. Even if it doesn't work out and you find you mismeasured, you can still use it for laundry detergent.

Once the test comes back clear, then you are ready to move into the finishing stages. Boil 40 ounces of distilled or filtered water on the stove in a large pot with a lid. Add all of the soap paste and stir. You may need the potato masher again. Once the soap paste is completely incorporated, you can turn off the heat and place the lid on the pot. Wait for an hour, then stir again. If it has a chunky or goopy consistency, then allow it to sit a little longer.

Once the mixture is smooth, you need to neutralize it with a mixture of borax in water. Dissolve one ounce of borax in two ounces of boiling water. It is important to keep it hot at this point. Weigh out two ounces of this mix and add it to the soap base in 1/2 ounce increments. Once it is entirely mixed in, you can choose to add any color or essential oils that you want. You should ideally only add two to three ounces.

THE REST PERIOD

Now you want to use the ladle to move your soap into the large jar. A gallon size glass jar is often best. Secure the lid and allow it to rest for a week or so. This allows solid particles to settle on the bottom. Once your soap is clear, pour it into smaller portions, label correctly and you are ready to go. Just make sure you don't disturb the settlement on the bottom otherwise you'll have to wait for it to settle completely again.

This will give you your liquid base soap to use for shampoo, body wash, dish soap, hand soap or any other projects you can think of. Now let's consider some specific liquid soap projects you can try.

Shampoo and Conditioner

Not only is liquid shampoo and conditioner cost-effective and natural to make, but it is also easy to create. When you make your own shampoos and conditioners, you don't have to worry about toxic chemicals that most commercial products have. Let's consider some shampoo and conditioner treatments that you can make at home.

BASIC SHAMPOO

Making your own shampoo is very simple. Simply take an empty bottle and fill it with equal parts distilled water and unscented liquid castile soap. Add a few drops of your preferred essential oil, and you're ready to go. You can also choose to experiment with other ingredients like honey, jojoba gel, aloe vera, dried herbs and even beer to create different mixes for specific types of hair.

A good basic recipe to start with and tweak as desired is the following:

- ✓ 2 tablespoons liquid castile soap
- ✓ 1 cup water
- ✓ 1/4 cup fresh herbs
- ✓ 1 teaspoon carrier oil
- ✓ 2 drops essential oil

Clarifying Shampoo

If you have been using a hair product for a while or have a lifestyle that leads to a pollutant build up in your hair, then a clarifying shampoo can be a great way to cleanse your hair through use once or twice a month. Simply mix one to two cups of warm water with one tablespoon of baking soda and a teaspoon of apple cider vinegar. Applying this to your hair and allowing it to sit for a few minutes is an excellent way to cleanse your hair. You can easily add essential oils of your choice.

Hair Mask

Coconut oil is a great way to create a simple and easy hair mask. Simply apply it directly to the hair from mid-shaft to the ends. Allow it to sit for a few minutes before rinsing. Doing this once or twice a week will help you to maintain healthy hair.

Dry Shampoo

If you don't have much time, you will be able to soap up unwanted oils in your hair with this option. A mix of coconut milk powder, cornmeal, baby powder and baking powder is all you need. The mix is based mostly on personal preference. A light dusting will provide an instant matte look that keeps your hair looking freshly washed.

Curl Enhancer

If you have curly hair, there is a natural way to maintain your curls. Mix together two tablespoons of aloe vera gel, two teaspoons of coconut oil and two tablespoons of shea butter. Apply about a tablespoon each day by twisting around your individual curls.

Frizz Tamer

Do you have a hard time dealing with flyaway hair? Coconut oil and olive oil are excellent options for this. Simply use a dime sized amount and lightly rub from mid-shaft to the ends of the hair to reduce frizz.

CONDITIONER

Making your own conditioner is just as easy as making shampoo. In addition to coconut and olive oil, you want to add a base ingredient such as plain yogurt, avocado or even bananas. If you want you can add honey, milk, herbs and essential oils to make the perfect conditioner combo. There are a few specific essential oil combinations you can use for specific hair types.

For greasy or oily hair and scalp, you should add six to eight drops of an essential oil like bergamot, lavender, lemon, rosemary, and sandalwood or tea tree.

For dry scalp and/or dandruff you should add six to eight drops of an essential oil like tea tree, peppermint, eucalyptus, lemon, and sage or rosemary.

Rosemary is a great essential oil for all hair types. Simply infuse vinegar by steeping several fresh rosemary sprigs in a few cups of apple cider vinegar for about one to two weeks. Strain out the rosemary and then use the vinegar to make the conditioner. The rosemary gives a great smell along with all the therapeutic benefits of rosemary. The other option is to add six to eight drops of rosemary essential oil to your conditioner for immediate use.

A good basic recipe to start with is the following:

- ✓ 2 ounces aloe vera gel
- ✓ 1/2 teaspoon carrier oil
- ✓ 2 ounces apple cider vinegar
- ✓ 1 ounce powdered milk

You don't have to stop only at making your own homemade shampoo and conditioner. You can also expand your recipe and project base to include homemade dog shampoos as well. Let's take a look at how you can do this.

Dog Shampoos

There are simple homemade dog shampoo recipes for all needs whether they are fleas or dry skin or somewhere in between. Dog grooming is becoming quite a big business, and many people will do anything for their pets. As with humans, many prefer to use natural and homemade shampoos for their dogs since they are healthier. Consider three main dog shampoo recipes that you can try.

COMMON INGREDIENTS

Two common components within any homemade dog shampoo are vinegar and baking soda. Other ingredients that you can customize include the carrier oil and glycerin. The most common carrier oil that is used is Castile soap, which is olive oil based. Some people choose to incorporate a baby shampoo or nontoxic dish soap in order to bind the ingredients. No matter what ingredients you choose, homemade dog shampoo recipes are simple and require very minimal preparation.

Flea Shampoo

There are plenty of recipes when it comes to homemade dog flea shampoo. One recipe is great for fleas, but also works for dogs with sensitive skin:

✓ One quart water.

✓ One cup white vinegar or apple cider vinegar.

✓ One cup baby shampoo or nontoxic dish soap.

If you have a smaller dog or puppy and want a smaller volume then you can try the following recipe:

✓ 1/2 cup water.

✓ 1/4 cup white vinegar or apple cider vinegar.

✓ 1/4 cup baby shampoo or nontoxic dish soap.

Either solution can be applied with a spray bottle or in a condiment bottle. Work the shampoo into the fur and allow it to soak for at least five minutes before rinsing. While it is soaking, you can comb or brush the dog to remove dead fleas.

Dry Shampoo

If you bathe your dog more often than once a month, you might dry out their skin. In between baths the dog's natural hair and skin chemistry takes into effect. A good solution between baths is to use a homemade dry dog shampoo. Most of these shampoos use baking soda. Massaging a dry shampoo into your dog's skin will often be easier than a wet bath. A typical dry dog shampoo includes the following:

✓ One cup baking soda.

✓ One cup corn starch.

✓ A few drops of essential oils, lemon, and lavender, are the most popular options.

Sprinkle the mixture on your dog and massage it into the skin with your hands or with a comb or brush. You should avoid using too much baking soda at a time; about a cup for a mid-sized dog and a half cup for a small dog or puppy. You should also avoid applying this mix too often since the residue can accumulate.

Itch Relief Shampoo

If you need to bathe your dog more frequently because of sensitive, itchy or dry skin, then you may want to consider making a homemade dog shampoo that provides relief. These shampoos often use aloe vera gel or glycerin. The recipe often includes the following:

✓ One quart water.
✓ One cup baby shampoo or nontoxic dish soap.
✓ One cup white vinegar or apple cider vinegar.
✓ 1/3 cup glycerin.
✓ Two tablespoons aloe vera gel.

Trying any of these options provides you with a cost-effective and healthy way to wash your dog.

Getting back to humans, what about cleaning your body? Let's consider how you can make your own liquid body wash at home.

Body Wash

If you want to enjoy a refreshing all-over clean feeling, then consider making your own homemade body wash. While a bar of soap can give you the same results, a homemade body wash is simple to make and can be customized to your unique body type. A homemade body wash is great a moisturizing your skin but is also gentle enough to use on your face. Not to mention if you have sensitive skin like mine, then you already know what commercial soaps can do to your skin. I am the living proof of that. Let's consider how you can make your own body wash and what goes into it.

Ingredients

All homemade body washes have some common ingredients. Consider the following elements that are most popular when making a homemade body wash.

Honey

Honey is a secret ingredient in most body wash recipes. Honey offers many benefits for the body whether it is used on the inside or outside. Through the use of honey, the body is able to retain moisture and elasticity. This makes honey a great ingredient for mature, dry, itchy or damaged skin. It is also a great ingredient to help increase the healing process for blemished skin.

While you may think honey would make a body wash sticky, it actually makes it smooth. However, you want to make sure you use raw and unfiltered honey.

Liquid Castile Soap

Pure liquid castile soap is what provides your homemade body wash with suds, so you don't have to add chemical foaming agents. You can choose to use the scented or unscented variety. If you are using scented castile soap, then you won't need to add essential oils unless you want them for therapeutic benefits. It is important to note that peppermint castile soap can be a bit tingly for sensitive skin areas.

Oil

In order to make a moisturizing body wash you need to add an oil that is easily absorbed by the skin. Two of the most popular options are jojoba and grapeseed oil. You may even find you don't need an additional moisturizer after using a body wash with these ingredients.

Vitamin E Oil

This ingredient is not only moisturizing but also repairing. It is rich in antioxidants, which can also help it to increase the shelf life of your personal care products. It is a great ingredient to add to summer or winter personal care products since your skin is more exposed to extreme temperatures and weather in these months.

Essential Oils

There are plenty of essential oils that are useful for a variety of skin conditions. Some essential oils can soothe, repair, heal, disinfect and deodorize skin. Carefully choose the essential oils you want to add to your body wash in order to get both therapeutic benefits as well as a pleasant scent.

Body Wash Recipe

Ingredients:

- ✓ 2/3 cup liquid castile soap, scented or unscented.

- ✓ 1/4 cup raw, unfiltered honey.

- ✓ 2 teaspoons oil of your choice.

- ✓ 1 teaspoon Vitamin E oil.

- ✓ 50-60 drops essential oils if desired of your choice.

Directions:

Carefully measure out all your ingredients and combine into a bottle with a squirt top. Shake well to mix initially and then shake gently before each use. To use either squirt into a washcloth, bath poof or directly onto your body. Since there is no water in this recipe, it will last up to a year. If your honey is creamy or thick, then you may need to warm it a bit in order to liquefy it before combining with the other ingredients. The main thing is to make sure you have a thorough mixing of all the ingredients.

Best Essential Oils for Skin

When it comes to adding essential oils to your body wash you both want to find a scent you enjoy while also keeping various skin types in mind. If you are going to use the body wash on children, babies or those with sensitive skin you may want to leave out essential oils or simply add a few drops of a mild essential oil such as chamomile or lavender. If children are going to use the body wash you should make sure you use half the suggested amount of essential oils.

You can have fun experimenting with various essential oils and combining for unique scents and therapeutic effects. Consider the following essential oils that are good for the skin:

German or Roman Chamomile - This is good for dry and sensitive skins, acne, eczema, and dermatitis.

Geranium - This is good for oily skin, acne, mature skin, eczema, dermatitis and other skin conditions. It can also help revitalize and brighten dull skin.

Grapefruit - This is good for toning the skin and is an extreme cleanser for oily skin.

Lavender - This is a gentle essential oil that is safe for all skin types, including sensitive skin. It works for mature skin, acne, eczema and psoriasis. It can also be an excellent soother for itchy skin.

Palmarosa - This essential oil can help stimulate new cell growth, moisturize skin and regulate oil production. This makes it an excellent essential oil for a variety of homemade skin products.

Patchouli - This essential oil works as an antimicrobial, astringent, fungicidal and deodorant. It works on acne, cracked and chapped skin as well as eczema, oily skin, and mature skin.

Peppermint - This is a very potent essential oil so you should only use half the recommended amount. It is cooling, refreshing and stimulating along with astringent properties. This makes it the perfect addition for acne.

Rosemary - This is a stimulating and restorative essential oil. It works for acne, eczema, and dermatitis. It should be avoided during pregnancy and by those with epilepsy or high blood pressure.

Sandalwood - This essential oil is useful for acne, dry, cracked or chapped skin. It can also be used on the mature skin to help with wrinkles.

Sweet Orange - This is one of the few citrus essential oils that is not phototoxic. It works for the dull and oily skin.

Tea Tree - This essential oil is antibacterial and can blend well with other essential oils such as lavender and peppermint. It can work for acne, oily skin, rashes and inflamed skin. However, too much of this oil will cause a drying effect. It will require some experimenting to find the right amount of this essential oil to use in a body wash.

This isn't an exhaustive list of essential oils to use in a body wash. Feel free to experiment with any essential oils that smell good and feature the properties you're looking for. If you need extra cleansing power, then let's consider making a homemade body scrub.

Body Scrub

In the winter months, the cold weather makes a moisturizing and exfoliating scrub a great product. There are a number of sugars, Epsom salt, carrier oil and essential oil combinations that can make excellent body scrubs. You can experiment with a number of ingredients, but the basic recipe you need to start with is the following:

Recipe

- ✓ 2 cups Epsom salts or sugar of your choice.
- ✓ 1 cup carrier oil of your choice; popular choices are grapeseed, olive, sweet almond, sesame, and safflower.
- ✓ 8 to 10 drops of your choice of essential oil.

Directions

Add the Epsom salts or sugar to a bowl and then slowly stir in the carrier oil until the mixture becomes smooth and not goopy. You may find you don't need to use the full cup of oil. Add the essential oil and other additions and mix until well combined. Spoon the mixture into a container or jar with a tight-fitting lid.

The products you can make with this recipe are endless. However, it is important to note that sometimes olive oil isn't the best carrier oil since it does have a strong scent. If you think olive oil may overpower the scent of a body scrub then either choose a different carrier oil or a stronger essential oil. If you want a fine grain scrub, you'll want to use sugar while Epsom salts give you a larger grain body scrub.

Sunburn Lotion

If you have fair skin and spend time outdoors in the summer, then you are likely to experience sunburn a time or two. Even if you diligently apply sunscreen, you may still find yourself with some degree of sunburn. If you want chemical-free relief from your sunburn, then consider making your own soothing, sunburn treatment lotion.

Ingredients

The first ingredient you need is a quality, natural aloe vera product. You should find one that is as close to natural as possible and is free of preservatives and chemicals. After you have a good aloe vera product, you next need to choose an oil that will nourish and repair your skin without causing additional irritation. Some good options to consider are red palm oil, coconut oil, and shea butter.

Red Palm Oil

This is often one of the most overlooked oils when it comes to homemade personal care products. This is because it is more expensive than coconut and olive oils. Although it can well be worth the extra money since it offers many skin healing benefits. It is very high in Vitamin E, medium chain triglycerides, carotene, healthy fats, and antioxidants. All of these mean that red palm oil is able to penetrate deep into the skin and heal from the base of the skin to the very top layer.

Coconut Oil

This is also great for the skin in many of the same ways as red palm oil. It is an ingredient that will help maintain moisture balance and promote skin cell regeneration.

Shea Butter

This is a luxurious, moisturizing ingredients for homemade personal care products such as sunburn, skin peeling and burns as a result of exposure to excessive heat. This ingredient will help reduce inflammation while providing extra vitamins and nutrients to improve overall skin health.

It also penetrates the skin well to moisturize effectively.

When it comes to sunburn relief, two excellent essential oil options to consider are lavender and helichrysum. Lavender is known to heal burns and ease the pain, while also helping to support cell regeneration.

Helichrysum has a pleasant honey-like scent that is useful for burns, wounds, bruises and other minor scratches and rashes. This essential oil can also help return moisture to the skin and reduce the pain associated with sunburn.

Recipe

✓ 1-ounce coconut oil

✓ 1-ounce red palm oil

✓ 2 ounces shea butter

✓ 2 ounces aloe vera gel

✓ 20 drops helichrysum essential oil

✓ 10 drops lavender essential oil

1. In a small jar combine the coconut oil, red palm oil, and shea butter.

2. Microwave in 30-second intervals until the oils become soft and are easy to mix; not quite liquid consistency.

3. Stir the ingredients well.

4. Add in the aloe vera gel and stir well.

5. Add in the essential oils and give a final stir.

6. If the ingredients seem too loose, then continue to stir and allow the oils to harden. In the end, the lotion should be soft, and a little bit will go a long way.

7. Allow the ingredients to cool completely. It can be stored in the refrigerator for one to two months.

Just because this recipe is meant for a sunburn treatment doesn't mean you only have to use it for that. This lotion actually works on a number of different burns and irritations, plus it has a sweet scent. Some other possible uses include the following:

- ➤ Kitchen burns

- ➤ Diaper rash

- ➤ Bug bites

- ➤ Chafing

- ➤ Rug burns

- ➤ Inflamed skin

On the other hand, if you simply need something to help with sore or stiff muscles then you can consider making a homemade balm. Let's take a look at this recipe next.

Muscle/Joint Balm

Whether it is a particular time of the year, maybe it is your regular workout made you sore or maybe you had a long day at work; we all get stiff joints and muscles at times. While warm water baths with Epsom salt can help ease the pain association with stiff joints and muscles, but most people want something that lasts longer.

Herbs and Spices that Help

If you are trying to create something for pain and stiffness under the skin, you are going to need to take a different approach than you would for something like hand cream. Hand cream is supposed to sit on the surface of your skin and then work into the top layer of the skin.

For a warming balm to work on sore muscles and joints, it needs to get below the skin. There are a few herbs and spices that can help get the active ingredients below the skin. Consider the following for use in your homemade balm.

SWEET BIRCH

This diluted essential oil is perfect for warming and healing stiff joints. It is often used in liniments for both humans and horses. Wintergreen essential oil is also similar since they both contain methyl salicylates, which is a mild pain reliever. Sometimes birch twigs will even be used in saunas to loosen stiff muscles.

CAYENNE

This acts as a stimulant that will loosen stiff muscles. It also has a lot of antioxidants which allows it to work as an anti-inflammatory.

GINGER

This plant works as a warming agent that will loosen stiff joints.

CINNAMON

This spice works in ways similar to the ginger plant but is milder for those who may not be able to tolerate ginger.

WILLOW BARK

The best source is white willow which contains a mild pain reliever.

Olive Oil

You can use this as a carrier oil or alone. It is a good ingredient due to its high levels of antioxidants.

Magnesium

This is a good muscle relaxant that will help relieve any pain associated with tense muscles.

Menthol

This is a great ingredient with anti-inflammatory properties, but may be a little strong for some.

Black Pepper

Adding this spice can help improve circulation.

Peppermint Essential Oil

This ingredient offers an excellent soothing and cooling effect.

ARNICA

This popular ingredient will help with soreness and bruise. However, this ingredient should never be used on broken skin.

NETTLES

Lastly, using this plant provides you with a number of vitamins, minerals, and antioxidants that are beneficial to sore muscles and joints.

Recipe Ingredients

To make this homemade balm, you are going to need infused oils. This is an easy process but will require a little extra time. If you don't have the time to make infused oils you can use essential oils, we'll discuss more on this later. First, let's look at the ingredients you need to make this homemade balm.

✓ Pint jar with lid

- ✓ 1 cup dried herbs or spices of your choice from the list above, you can mix if you want
- ✓ 1 cup of carrier oil; the most popular options are olive, grapeseed, safflower, and sunflower
- ✓ Beeswax pellets or any other type of wax you have on hand

Directions

To make an infused oil do the following:

1. Place the dried herbs in the pint jar. If you use moist, fresh herbs, then carrier oils will go bad. Cover the dried herbs with the carrier oil. Secure the lid and then shake the jar a few times.

2. Place the jar in a sunny location and leave it for a few weeks while shaking daily.

3. After two to three weeks your oil should have turned very dark. This is when you'll strain it. You can use a funnel or coffee filter depending on the size of your herbs. Allow it to sit for an hour or

more to allow all of the oil to run through the filter. After this, you can put together your balm.

4. Melt equal parts wax and infused oil in a double boiler. Once the wax is completely melted in the oil, stir it well to mix thoroughly.

5. Pour the mix into a shallow jar.

6. Allow it to sit and harden for a few hours. Once it is cool, test to see if you can easily get your fingers into it. If it is too hard, you can melt it down again in a pan of warm water and then add additional oil. You can melt it down a few times until you get the right consistency. You want a consistency that is firm, but easily melts when you put your fingers into it. If it is too soft, you can melt it down again and add more wax.

When using the balm, simply spread it on the affected joints or muscles. Remember to wash your hands after using the balm since some of the herbs and spices in it can be an irritant to your eyes, nose or other sensitive areas. In some cases, it can even burn sensitive skin areas so use with caution.

Variations

If you don't have the time or ability to make infused oil, then you can simply use essential oils instead. Simply melt your wax and carrier oil together and then add a few drops of essential oil once the mixture is completely melted and cooled slightly. Some of the best essential oils to use when making this variation include the following:

✓ Peppermint

✓ Ginger

✓ Black Pepper

✓ Sweet Birch

✓ Wintergreen

Never use a combination of warm and cool oils.

Another option to help get the balm deep into your joints is to add emu oil. This is a transdermal oil that will help transport the carrier oil and essential oil deep under the skin where they can provide the most benefits. If you don't want to use emu oil you can also apply the balm with a warm wet towel. Rub the balm on the affected area and then cover with a warm, damp towel. Leave until the towel cools and then repeat the process.

Mosquito Repellent

Whether you are heading outside for a
summer retreat or simply want to enjoy your front

yard or patio; you'll likely be faced with an insect or two. While most will suggest you cover up to decrease your chance of getting bit, sometimes this isn't the best option in the summer when it's hot.

On the other hand, you can use commercial bug spray. However, this option often leads to you apply layers of chemicals on your skin while also releasing chemicals into the environment that can be inhaled or settle on your food.

If you don't like either of these options, then the good news is there is a third effective option. There are some essential oil options for creating mosquito repellent that are very successful without the heavy chemicals.

Do Your Research

If you're still on the fence about whether or not you want to discontinue use of commercial repellents than take a moment to do your research. Look up some information about DEET and other chemicals used in commercial repellents. Once you do your research, you'll likely be on the side of using a natural bug repellent that not only smells better but is also effective and easy to make. However, it is important that you know different essential oils will repel different types of bugs, so you will need to use a combination of essential oils to successfully ward off a variety of insects. Let's look at how you can create an effective bug repellent.

Ingredients

- ✓ 2 tablespoons of witch hazel and/or vodka.
- ✓ 2 tablespoons of a carrier oil; the most popular options are grapeseed, jojoba, almond, olive or neem oil. Neem oil contains some natural insecticidal compounds.
- ✓ 1/2 teaspoon vodka for a preservative if you aren't already using it above.
- ✓ 100-110 drops of essential oils.

ESSENTIAL OILS

As I said earlier, different oils are going to repel different bugs. Consider some of the following essential oils when picking a combination for your bug repellent.

One option is 55 drops lemon eucalyptus essential oil. Even the CDC has reported that this is a good natural substitute for DEET when repelling insects. However, it shouldn't be used for children under the age of three.

Another option is 15 drops of lavender essential oil. With this option, you want to explicitly use Lavandula Angustifolia since it has the best insecticidal qualities.

Two others options are 15 drops Cedar Wood or 15 drops Rosemary essential oils.

Other options you can experiment include the following:

* Citronella
* Eucalyptus
* Lemongrass
* Tea Tree
* Peppermint
* Cypress
* Rose Geranium
* Bergamot
* Lemon

Directions

First add your carrier liquids to a small spray bottle, ideally a three to four-ounce bottle, so you have room to shake the ingredients. Next, add the essential oils. Shake the bottle well before each application. For maximum effectiveness, you will need to reapply the natural bug repellent every few hours.

Tips and Warnings

As with all essential oil products, always make sure you talk to a health practitioner before using if you are pregnant or nursing.

Always use caution when using essential oils on young children.

If it is your first time using essential oils, perform a patch test on your skin to check for an allergic reaction before using it over a large area of your body.

Make sure all homemade products are properly labeled.

When making a product such as an insect repellent made from essential oils, make sure you place them in a dark colored bottle and store it in a cool, dark place.

Hand Scrub

By now if you showed enough interest into making homemade products; then chances are you spend a lot of time outdoors in your garden. Of perhaps you have a job where your hands get dirty.

It is important to make sure you can get your hands as clean as possible before preparing any food. An excellent solution for this is a homemade hand scrub. Not only will this cleanse your hands, but it will also exfoliate the skin to keep your hands moisturized.

Ingredients

It is easy to find all of the ingredients you need for a homemade hand scrub at a local craft or grocery store. This recipe is also easy to customize so you can easily experiment with other ingredients and make a variety of products to add to your product line.

The most popular exfoliant ingredients for a hand scrub are dried rose petals, apricot kernel, and sugar. All three of these ingredients are mild abrasives that help to remove grime and dirt gently. Rose petals will also help to calm inflammation.

When it comes to a carrier oil, one of the most popular options is the moisturizing sweet almond oil. This oil is easily absorbed into the skin and has a high amount of antioxidants such as Vitamin E. Sweet almond oil helps to restore moisture balance to the skin while also exfoliating the pores and removing dirt.

For a hand scrub, I prefer a night subtle garden scent like rose. So I often add a geranium essential oil. This oil not only has a nice subtle scent, but it is also a skin healing oil that is anti-inflammatory. So while cleaning your hands, this essential oil will also boost your mood and improve stress and depression.

Variants

If you don't like the idea of a rose scent, then you can easily add your own essential oil options. For example, if you want a citrus scent you can consider using dried lemon or orange peels instead of rose petals and a lemon or orange essential oil in place of the geranium essential oil. Another option could be a lavender version by using dried lavender buds instead of rose petals and lavender essential oil in place of geranium essential oil. The possibilities for variants are truly endless with this recipe.

Recipe

- ✓ 1 cup sugar
- ✓ 1/4 cup dried rose petals
- ✓ 1/4 cup ground apricot kernel
- ✓ 1/3 cup sweet almond oil
- ✓ 10 drops geranium essential oil

DIRECTIONS

1. Crush the rose petals or another dried ingredient into small pieces.

2. Add dried ingredient, sugar and apricot seeds in a small bowl.

3. Stir all ingredients well.

4. Stir while pouring in the sweet almond oil.

5. Add in your choice of essential oil and stir well.

6. Transfer the ingredients to a dark, airtight container for storage.

When ready to use, scoop a small amount onto your hands. Gently work it into your fingertips and under nail beds. Then just rinse and dry your hands as you normally would. You should have some oil left over to moisturize your hands and prevent over-drying.

The hand scrub can be stored in an airtight, dark colored container for one to two months.

Hand Sanitizer

With disease and sicknesses on the rise, hand sanitizers are becoming a mainstay for people at home and at work. You'll often find hand sanitizers in a number of strategic locations. Traditional hand washing requires thirty seconds that some may not have on a busy day. Commercial hand sanitizers often have a heavy chemical scent that sticks to your hands all day. If you want a better alternative, then consider making your own hand sanitizer.

There are plenty of essential oil options that offer you all the benefits of an antibacterial, antiviral and antifungal hand sanitizer. Let's look at how you can make your own hand sanitizer.

Ingredients

- ✓ 5-10 drops lavender essential oil or other essential oil of your choice
- ✓ 30 drops tea tree essential oil or other essential oil of your choice
- ✓ 1 tablespoon witch hazel extract or high-proof vodka
- ✓ 8 ounces 100% pure aloe vera gel
- ✓ 1/4 teaspoon Vitamin E oil to increase shelf life and soften hands

Directions

Add the essential oils and Vitamin E oil to a small glass bowl or container and swirl to mix entirely. Add the witch hazel or vodka and swirl again. Combine to the aloe vera gel and mix well. The sanitizer will last several months when you add Vitamin E and alcohol to preserve. Shake the ingredients gently before each use. You can make it more portable by transferring it to small, clean squirt bottles. It is best to use dark colored bottles to prevent exposing the essential oils to light.

Warnings and Tips

If you are going to use lavender in the recipe, it will help to tone down the strong scent of the tea tree oil. If you don't want to use lavender then you should choose another essential oil with antibacterial properties. Some other good options include rosemary, sage, sandalwood or peppermint.

As we've discussed, always use caution when handling essential oils. Always test for an allergic reaction before applying to large areas of your skin.

Face Mask

A good face mask has two main components, but everything you need is likely already in your kitchen. One thing a face mask needs is to be able to stick to your face. The other thing is the base that will determine the benefits the face mask provides. Let's look at some of the most common bases and their benefits.

AVOCADO

Avocado is a great base option. It has the texture needed to stay on your face, but it also provides excellent moisturizing benefits. If you suffer from dry or overexposed skin, then you should use an overripe avocado to make a face mask.

OATMEAL

If you grew up when chicken pox was common then you have likely found yourself taking an oatmeal bath. This is because oatmeal will help soothe irritated skin. In addition, oatmeal acts as a cleanser to remove built-up oils and impurities in your skin and will exfoliate as you scrub it off your skin. You can use oatmeal in your face mask either in the cooked or uncooked state.

PLAIN YOGURT

This is one of the most popular options for a homemade face mask. The cool, smooth texture not only feels great on your skin; but it is also one of the easiest to keep on your skin. Yogurt also offers a number of benefits for your skin. It is moisturizing, antibacterial and has lactic acid which is very helpful for your skin.

Egg Whites

Lastly, this is one of the less common options for a face mask. Most people find the texture of raw eggs off-putting, so it doesn't get used as a face mask ingredient too often. However, they are a good option if you want an ingredient that will tighten skin and reduce pore size.

In addition to your base ingredients, you also want to consider some add-ins. Let's look at some of the best and most popular options.

Cocoa Powder

Cocoa powder is an ingredient that is known for high antioxidant properties and provides an excellent boost to your skin. It also allows your face mask to smell great.

HONEY

Honey is by far the most popular ingredient in face masks. It has a sticky texture and adhesive properties, making it a great natural ingredient for face masks. It also features antibacterial properties that can help with acne while also cleansing the skin. Lastly, for those with dry skin; honey can act as a moisturizer.

LEMON JUICE

This is the last potential add-in ingredient for your face mask. It features both antibacterial and antifungal properties. With regular application, it can help brighten your skin and help bleach dark spots.

Recipes

There are many ways to combine the ingredients above into a face mask. Simply mix the ingredients you want and apply to your face. Keep the mask on for twenty minutes and then wash off with cool water. Consider the following best recipes and then consider your own combinations.

SKIN BOOST:

- ✓ 2 tablespoons plain yogurt
- ✓ 1 tablespoon honey
- ✓ 1 tablespoon cocoa powder

SKIN MOISTURIZER

- ✓ 1/2 an avocado
- ✓ 1 tablespoon honey
- ✓ 1 teaspoon lemon juice

SKIN TIGHTENING AND PORE REDUCTION

- ✓ 1 egg white

- ✓ 1 tablespoon lemon juice

IRRITATED SKIN SOOTHER

- ✓ 1/2 cup oatmeal
- ✓ 1 tablespoon honey

These are just a few simple recipes to get you started, but you can easily experiment with your own combination.

Now that we've discussed some of the more popular skin care products you can make let's look at the business aspect and what goes into starting your own skin care business.

PART – 2

How to Start, Run & Grow Your New Business

Deciding to Start Your New Soap Business

Soap making isn't that difficult to do, but it does take time to master. How do you know when you've mastered soap making? There is a lot of time and research that goes into getting your business started, but you never really stop learning and improving your soap making craft.

When it comes to soap making; **there isn't any mandated testing, governing body or federal certification needed as with other professions.** So how can you know when your soap products are ready to take to market?

Soap making is a constant learning process. There are many elements involved that you may not have considered. Mastering soap making won't happen overnight, but if you keep trying you'll succeed. First, you'll need to watch the professional. Then you can start getting your hands on learning. You can either take soap making classes in your area or learn from another professional in the area.

Once you have the basics down, it is time to do some research. You want to research ingredients so you can study and formulate ideas for products. Do you know the properties of all the possible carrier oils? Using the right combination of ingredients can make the difference between a great soap product and a terrible product. After a lot of trial and error, you'll start to perfect formulas that are worthy of selling.

The next step is to test your soap recipes. This is an important step. After you've designed a recipe that you feel is perfect, you want to test and retest it. Ask your friends and family to volunteer. While these people will most willing help, they may not offer you the most honest critique. Look for sources that will give you an honest opinion and view negative critique as a way to improve.

While you start testing your soap, you can start looking into ways to incorporate your business. Do you want to be a sole proprietor, a limited liability company (LLC) or any of the other type of incorporations? Go to the Small Business Administration (SBA) for advice and resources that can help you make the right decision. This is also a good time to start looking into your insurance options. Product liability insurance not only protects your customers but also your assets. You can often get pointed in the right direction from a homeowner's insurance broker.

After this, you may be ready to start selling your soaps. However, before we get into the specifics of starting a business; let's take a moment to make sure you are ready to start a small business. Let's consider five things to ask yourself before starting a small business.

5 Questions to Ask to Make Sure You're Ready

Ask yourself why you started making soaps in the first place. Was it for relaxation? Was it to give meaningful gifts to others? A way to let out your creativity? You may have more than one reason for making soaps. Perhaps you always thought of turning your soap making into a business, or maybe you are just now thinking about it.

You should certainly be aware that starting a small business is a challenge. Get started by considering the following five questions to make sure you are in the right position to start a small business of making soaps.

IS THE PROCESS STILL ENJOYABLE WHEN DICTATED BY A DEADLINE?

People often get into soap making as a creative hobby or a leisure activity for relaxation. However, when you start a small business, it is no longer a leisure activity. You won't be able to be doing it as an art project; rather you are going to be producing certain items that need to be made on a regular basis by a specific deadline. If you have a schedule based on consumer demand, how will you feel about your soap making venture?

HOW WILL YOU FEEL DOING IT UNDER THE PRESSURE OF FINANCIAL DEMANDS?

Turning a hobby into business requires a lot of expenses. You may need to quit your current full-time job, hire a babysitter so you can focus on growing your business. You'll also need the necessary funds to buy bulk supplies, rent a warehouse, build a website and set up marketing efforts. In the beginning, you may even be putting more money into your business than you are getting back and this can cause a lot of stress.

This can make a big psychological difference between doing a fun hobby and running a business that needs to pay the bills. If you think turning your hobby into a business means you'll still be able to have fun you may be in for a big surprise. Consider how the financial pressure and time pressure are going to change your experience. This isn't to say that running a business can't be fun. But a new venture startup is usually an uphill battle at first.

IS YOUR HOBBY MEANT FOR RELAXATION?

Once you start a home business, it's likely you won't find your hobby to have a relaxing effect. There are definitely other rewards, but relaxation may not be the main one. This means you might need to find another outlet for your stress. On top of it, you'll need to find a way to balance your time between running the business and doing your new outlet for the stress.

ARE YOU READY TO BE A CEO?

Just because you are good at soap making, doesn't mean you are suited to other aspects of running a business. There is no doubt you have the skill and ability to create products that people want, but when you run a business, you are going to do a lot of other job duties as well. In fact, at some point, you might grow your business to the point that you hire others to make the soaps while you simply run the business.

Ask yourself if you know how to balance the books, market your products, work with social media, set appointments, deal with wholesalers and retailers and all the other many jobs that a business owner needs to do. If you aren't able to do these activities, do you have the time and effort to devote to learning how to do these activities?

ARE YOU WILLING TO BE A SALES PERSON?

When you first start, you'll likely do well at craft fairs and maybe even get one or two local stores to stock your product line. When you're at this early stage, your products will likely sell themselves. However, as you grow beyond this, you'll need to acquire customers and get attention from distribution outlets to ensure the success of your business. Are you willing to develop the persistence of a good sales person? You will need to shift from a creative skill set to a marketer skill set at this point in order for your business to survive, thrive and grow.

While these questions may cause you to question whether or not starting a small business is right for you, there are benefits involved. There is certainly a lot that goes into starting a small business, but it also offers a lot of benefits as well. Now I'm going to tell you about ten benefits and reasons why you should start a small business.

10 Benefits to Starting a Small Business

When it comes to starting a business, it is clear from our earlier discussion that it requires a lot of work. In fact, the statistics from the Small Business Administration shows that only half of new small businesses survive past the first five years and only a third beyond that survive to ten years.

However, this doesn't mean there isn't a positive side to starting a small business. Let's look at ten benefits you can enjoy if you decide to start your small business making liquid soaps.

YOU OFFER CUSTOMERS A BETTER CHOICE

There are a number of companies that offer new technologies and products that people haven't heard of before. While you don't need a revolutionary new product to start a small business, it helps if you have something that can help your product stand out from the competition. With soap making it is easy to make a better soap at a reasonable price that offers customers a better alternative to the commercial products with harsh chemicals in them.

YOU ARE OFFERING SOMETHING THAT'S IN DEMAND

Customers are always looking for great products. If you have specialized knowledge and experience in soap making, you will find it easier to sell your products to others. Unique, quality, homemade products are going to stand out in a commercial market filled with other options. When you offer value to your customers then will keep coming back for more. As a small business, it will be easier to react to customers changing preferences and anticipate future demands.

INDEPENDENCE AND FREEDOM

Perhaps the most attractive aspect of running a small business is the ability to be your own boss, especially if you've had less than ideal bosses before. While there are a certain degree of risks involved with running your own business, you can make your own decisions and decide how to control your business. Although you'll no longer have the comfort and security of a full-time job, you'll be able to call your own shots and gain your own financial independence.

DEVELOP YOUR PASSION

You likely know at least one person who truly enjoys their work. They are likely to be a very happy individual. Most who follow their passion aren't fortunate enough to get a job that fits them perfectly, but you can when you start your own business. A large part of your life is spent on the job. So if you enjoy an art such as soap making, then you should start a small business around that passion and follow your dream.

A PERSONAL CHALLENGE

When you start a business, then each day will bring a new set of challenges and experiences. You are going to be required to learn to be creative when solving problems and learn to work with various types of people. At times you'll need to learn the hard way too but again that is part of the whole learning experience. However, this will increase your personal confidence and help you improve your innovative thinking and decision making.

PERSONAL REWARDS

A lot of small business owners are attracted to the personal rewards they enjoy when doing hard work for themselves and not someone else. There is no limit to how much money you can make when you have your own small business. You will make all the decisions and face all the consequences. Knowing the future rests on your shoulders leads a lot of people to thrive and become successful.

SATISFACTION AND PRIDE

When you create a product or business from nothing, it comes with a lot of satisfaction and pride of accomplishment. These sensations are a motivating force when applying your skills to a small business. Building a successful small business and seeing it grow into a thriving company is a very rewarding experience that you won't get any other way. It is always nice to see returning customers who are choosing your products over others.

HAVING AN AGENDA

Although starting a small business means long hours; you'll ultimately be in control of how, when and where you work. Some small businesses never leave the home, and others grow into a large, thriving business. It is your choice alone as to the agenda your business is going to take. When you run your own business, you'll have choices that you normally won't have as an average employee. You can set your own priorities and make decisions that determine the nature, volume, and schedule of your work.

CONNECTING WITH PEOPLE

As an employee, you'll often work for a company and interact with the same people every day. When you own a small business, the experience is vastly different. You'll deal with a range of individuals from suppliers to customers. You'll eventually learn how to deal with all types of people and make excellent personal connections. You can also pick like minded people to surround yourself with.

SUPPORT THE COMMUNITY

Small businesses are the backbone of communities. You can help the local community grow in both stability and culture. Customers like to frequent businesses that give back to the local community. This also offers you the sense of pride in benefiting the community and helping those around you.

These are just a few of the most common benefits to starting your own small business making liquid soaps. Let's take a moment to summarize what we've just discussed before we look at what you need to do to start your own small business.

16 PERSONAL QUESTIONS YOU SHOULD ASK YOURSELF FIRST

As I've discussed the first thing you need to do is look closely at yourself and make sure you are ready to start your own small business. For this you want to ask yourself the following questions:

❖ Are you a self-starter with the discipline to work on your own?

❖ Are you able to avoid personal distractions when working at home and focus on business issues?

❖ Are you good at multi-tasking your time and priorities?

❖ Are you organized and efficient?

❖ Are you ready to take full responsibility for ensuring the success of a business?

❖ Are you able to devote the necessary time to build a business?

- Are you decisive and proactive, even if you don't have all the answers?

- Do you require a regular paycheck for security?

- Do you have the skills to negotiate aggressively?

- Do you work efficiently while under stress and deadlines?

- Do you have the drive and motivation to keep a business going even during difficult times?

- Do you have the ability to work with all types of people?

- Do you have the integrity and confidence to work with customers and suppliers?

- Do you have the business skills to balance the books?

- Do you have the drive to keep going, even when things aren't going your way?

- Do you have a take-charge attitude and perseverance that gets you to overcome problems and obstacles you may face?

Advantages and Disadvantages

If after answering these questions you still feel you can start a small business then you want to move on to considering the advantages and disadvantages of a small business. Let's look at both in a simple breakdown.

Advantages:

✧ You'll be doing something you really want with your life.

✧ You'll be your own boss in control of your company and future.

✧ You'll enjoy all the rewards from your hard work.

✧ You won't have to commute to work, which will save you both time and money.

✧ You'll have a sense of accomplishment and success.

✧ You'll be able to set your own work schedule.

Disadvantages:

- ✧ It may disrupt your family life at first.
- ✧ Your initial income may be significantly low.
- ✧ You'll need to make investments for initial equipment.
- ✧ You'll need to devote space in your home that may not be currently available.
- ✧ You'll need to devote a lot of hours to hard work which may include nights and weekends.
- ✧ You'll need to do multiple tasks and find the time to do all of them.

If you're ready to start your liquid soap making business, then let's consider how to start a home based business. The first step in starting your home business is to make sure you have all the legal aspects in place.

The Legal Aspects

In order to have a successful business, you need to have a strong foundation. To develop a strong foundation, you need a sound plan. With a lifestyle business like liquid soap, you want to keep it relatively simple. Consider the following five steps to help you develop a strong foundation for your business.

The first step is to make sure you research FDA guidelines and legal issues. Doing this will prevent you from making major mistakes. For example, you don't want to use any ingredients the FDA may question. Another thing many small businesses lack is liability insurance.

It isn't that costly and can protect you in the future. You should also speak with an experienced accountant about what you need to do in regards to incorporation, tax filing, and business registration. Having this information before you start your business is very important. The last thing to be prepared for is keeping batch records. In some situations this may be a legal requirement, but it is also good quality control and protects you and your business. You want to keep records of ingredients, amounts used and exactly how you prepared each batch.

Next, you need to give your new business a legal structure, so it becomes a real business. For this here are the few steps you need to be taking:

1. Name your business
2. Incorporate your business
3. Apply and obtain EIN number
4. Apply for all local, city, county and State regulatory licenses
5. Open a commercial bank account

Naming your business is most likely one of the most important parts of your business. There are two names you have to come up with. One is your brand's name, and other is your legal entity name.

Next, you have to prepare your articles of incorporation and file. Your attorney or your accountant can help you in this matter.

Often you have the option of choosing to file as a limited liability company or LLC, general partnership or even sole proprietorship. A sole proprietorship is the ideal business structure for someone starting a home based business, especially if it is a moderate start from you home. However, most prefer the benefits of an LLC.

If you plan to eventually expand your business to retail locations or potentially online, then you definitely don't want to file as a sole proprietor. In this instance, you should definitely file as an LLC.

When you file as an LLC, you will be able to protect yourself from personal liability. This means that if anything goes wrong while operating your business then only the money you invested into the company is at risk. This isn't the case if you file as a sole proprietor or a general partnership. LLCs are simple and flexible to operate since you won't need a board of directors, shareholder meetings or other managerial formalities in order to run your business.

Here are all the legal business structures you can choose from, it is best to get some advice from your CPA or accountant or an attorney.

Business Structure

When starting a business, there are five different business structures you can choose from:

✧ Sole Proprietor

✧ Partnership

✧ Corporation (Inc. or Ltd.)

✧ S Corporation

❖ Limited Liability Company (LLC)

Sole Proprietor

This is not the safest structure for a growing soap or personal care business. It is used for a business owned by a single person or a married couple. Under this structure, the owner is personally liable for all business debts and may file on their personal income tax.

Partnership

This is another inexpensive business structure to form. It often requires an agreement between two or more individuals who are going to jointly own and operate a business.

The partners will share all aspects of the business in accordance with the agreement. Partnerships don't pay taxes, but they need to file an informational return. Individual partners then report their share of profits and losses on their personal tax returns.

Corporation (Inc. or Ltd.)

This is one of the more complex business structures and has the most startup costs of any business structure. It isn't a very common structure among used car businesses since there are shares of stocks involved.

Profits are taxed both at the corporate level and again when distributed to shareholders. When you structure a business at this level, there are often lawyers involved.

S CORPORATION

This is one of the most popular types of business entity people forms to it avoid double taxation. It is taxed similarly to a partnership entity. But an S Corp. needs to be approved to be classified as such.

LIMITED LIABILITY COMPANY (LLC)

This is the most common business structure among most small businesses. It offers lots of benefits for small businesses since it reduces the risk of losing all your personal assets in case you are faced with a lawsuit. It provides a clear separation between business and personal assets. You can also elect to be taxed as a corporation, which saves you money come tax time.

If you are unsure which specific business structure you should choose then, you can discuss it with an accountant. They will direct you in the best possible option for what your business goals are.

A sample article of incorporation for an LLC entity is attached at the end of this book for reference only.

EIN NUMBER FROM IRS

EIN or Employer Identification number is essentially a social security or tax identification number but for your business. IRS and many other governmental agencies can identify your business via this unique 9 digit number.

Remember you will not need this number if you choose to be a sole proprietorship for your business.

It is simple to apply, either you can do it yourself or get your accountant to apply for you, but the process is simple, you fill out the form SS-4, which can be filed online, via Fax or via mail.

Here is a link to IRS website where you can download or fill out the form online.

https://www.irs.gov/businesses/small-businesses-self-employed/how-to-apply-for-an-ein

A sample EIN application is attached at the end of the book.

OPENING A COMMERCIAL BANK ACCOUNT

This is one important step, but it can only be done after you have a fully executed article of incorporation which has been approved by the state, and you have an EIN number assigned by the IRS.

Once you have these two documents, you should be able to go to a bank and open your first commercial bank account.

But remember to check and understand various types of commercial checking account fees, you want to find a bank that offers free or almost free commercial checking account because some larger banks can charge you hundreds of dollars each month depending on how many transactions you do. Make sure to ask and shop around before you sign on the dotted line.

The next step is to establish your brand and what makes you unique. Ask yourself what could make people prefer your products over others? The cosmetics field has a lot of competition, and you need your brand to stand out from the rest. However, this competition is good since the larger brands help generate interest and awareness among the public.

Learn from the findings of others' market research. Just make sure you put a creative spin on your product or message. After you identified your unique value and chosen a strong company name, you want to focus on quality logos and packaging designs. Having a logo professionally designed is certainly an investment that pays you back for years to come.

Next, you want to test your brand for customer opinion and interest. A good place to start is with family and friends, but keep in mind they may not give you an unbiased opinion. After you have a few recipes that follow FDA guidelines you can consider a sampling campaign.

This will both tell you people's interest in your product and general consumer interest. Be creative with your options; some popular choices are house parties, focus groups, and crowd funding. The main thing is to find a targeted audience that will give you honest and unbiased feedback.

The fourth step is to have a solid marketing plan. Simply having a website doesn't mean you'll sell products. You need to have a proven marketing strategy. Ask yourself: what set of activities draw customers to your products? There are plenty of possibilities including craft shows, retail stores, Amazon or Etsy. Blogging often and using online strategies to build up your website. If needed consider group or self-study courses that teach you about online marketing.

Let's look at these areas in more depth to help you see what goes into each of them. The first thing to consider is how to create a strong business plan, as this is the foundation for any successful business.

Creating a Strong Business Plan

The key to having a successful business is to develop a strong business plan. A business plan allows you to understand the marketplace and how to set your business apart from the competition. In this section, we'll look at the common elements and what you need to include in your business plan.

Starting a business without a solid plan is not only a risk, but most banks won't provide you with a loan without first seeing a solid business plan. A business plan acts as a roadmap for establishing and running a business.

While banks are interested in what you have to offer and how you plan to sell, it all comes down to how you'll manage the money from the loan. A bank wants to see solid evidence that you've thought about everything before they are willing to commit money to your endeavor. A solid business plan doesn't have to be complicated, but it does need to be thorough.

BUSINESS SUMMARY

The first section is focused on providing a top-level summary of your business and needs to grab the reader's attention. This section needs basic information such as the following:

✓ Formation date

✓ Description of products

✓ Key personnel

✓ Number of employees

✓ Location

✓ Mission statement

✓ Reasons for success

The financial information is going to be determined by the stage of your business. If you have an established business, then you can rely on the historical financial date that includes growth over time, sales, profits, and market share. Portraying this data in graph format is very helpful. If you have a startup, then you need to rely on projections of future performance that uses realistic and dependable assumptions.

Growth prospects are important for any size business since investors focus largely on their potential return on investment. Provide an outline of your goals and plans for where the company will go in the future. While attracting the widest possible audience, you also want to make it concise and informative.

BUSINESS DESCRIPTION

In this section, you are going to explain the nature of your business. Make sure you describe all the critical elements that make your business unique and can lead to your success. List and evaluate both a primary and secondary target market. Show how your products are going to satisfy the needs of these markets. Identify what types of consumers you plan to serve and what allows you to stand out from the competition. Ideally you need to find a niche with in the market and own that niche, rule that niche, become the authority figure within that niche.

BUSINESS MANAGEMENT

This section is going to be easy if you're starting a small business out of your home. First, identify the type of ownership along with your personal background and education. If you are going to have employees, you'll need to describe their organizational structure along with the role and qualifications of each employee.

Explain all salary and benefits packages along with promotional opportunities. If you are going to use contract labor or outside advisers you'll also need to explain their roles and pay structure.

Ownership information needs to include the following:

✓ Names

✓ Type and amount of equity stake

✓ Level of involvement

✓ Background and experience

✓ Track record

✓ Notable achievements

✓ Primary responsibilities

✓ Compensation

✓ Years with the company

✓ Unique skills

✓ How they contribute to the businesses' success

PRODUCTS

This is where you'll provide details on the products you intend to sell. You'll want to place emphasis on the products that benefit your target customers. Discuss any research activities, new products in development and how you plan to stand out from the competition. You'll want to explain the life cycles of all products or how they go from ideas to marketable products.

Be sure to list any intellectual property, trade secrets, trademarks, copyrights and patents whether they are already granted or in the works. Also explain any legal agreements such as sole-source provider, non-compete agreements or nondisclosure agreements.

MARKETING STRATEGIES

In this section, you'll want to focus on market analyses and the strategies you'll employ to capitalize on your target markets. You should include statistical data that shows the following:

✓ Market size

✓ Historical growth rates

✓ Current market trends

✓ Competitive landscape

- ✓ Target customer demographics
- ✓ Purchasing trends
- ✓ Forecast growth
- ✓ Projected market share
- ✓ Pricing structure

The competitive analysis needs to provide a realistic assessment of your strengths and weaknesses compared to the competition. Include any barriers to entry, market opportunities, technology hurdles, regulatory restrictions, employee pools and the importance of your targeted markets to your competitors.

After finishing your market analysis, you want to identify the management and sales strategies you'll use to maximize growth and profits. This includes all approaches to reaching target customers, social media, advertising campaigns, and promotions. Include any plans for acquisitions as you expand your business. Ideally, you should be focused on driving sales and building customer loyalty. Show how you plan to distribute and get your products on the market through methods such as retail stores, catalogs, websites and personal sales force.

FINANCING

This is likely the most important section of your business plan and where you'll want to focus the majority of your preparation time. If you've already been operating your business for a while, you'll want to have five years of balance sheets, cash flow data, and income statements.

If you plan to apply for a loan, you'll want to include a list of assets and potential collateral. You'll also want to include financial projections for the next five years including sales, profit margins, capital expenditures, operating income and expenses, and cash flow.

If you plan to apply for a loan, you should state a specific amount and timeframe for financial need.

Make sure it can be fully supported by the financial projections compiled. If you are going to spread the funding out over time, then you should provide a quarterly estimate summarized by each year. Explain exactly how the money is going to be used and why it is needed.

If there is anything that can affect your repayment of a loan, make sure you disclose it up front. The bank is going to do a risk assessment anyways, so you don't want to hide any information they are likely to find.

APPENDIX

This is a good section to put any additional information that is relevant or important. It is a good idea to keep it separate so you can give it to those who need to know. This could include additional documents such as the following:

✓ Reference letters

✓ Key contracts

✓ Leases

- ✓ Credit history
- ✓ Photographs
- ✓ Resumes
- ✓ Licenses
- ✓ Magazine articles (if any)
- ✓ Financial documents (Both personal & Business in applicable)
- ✓ Legal documents

Keep track of who you give the business plan to and the appendix. The business plan is key to the success of your business. Most small business experience failure due to insufficient capital and a good business plan is key to getting the financing you need.

In addition, the business plan provides you with a roadmap that keeps you on course should your business hit hard times. The business plan should provide you with a glimpse into the next three to five years of your business. Now that you have a business plan in place, the next step is to create a brand for your business.

Creating a Strong Brand around your Products

All products are worthy of a customer's attention, but the focus of your brand is to grab their attention. Often small business owners put all their passion and imagination into the soap itself and don't place the same drive and focus on their brand, which is actually the first thing prospective clients and investors see.

Branding means a lot more to your company than coming up with a logo and tagline. Rather the branding should be viewed as the identity of your company or the image of your company. Through your brand you are providing a unique voice for your company along with a memorable message for prospective customers.

Those with successful branding are the ones who are able to incorporate their values and mission into it. Your core message needs to have both a rational and emotional side in order to connect with people's minds and hearts completely.

What message do you want to present to the world? Are you passionate about a specific solution or cause? Bring your passion and significant values into all aspects of your company's brand. However, don't make it overly complex since a simple idea will resonate on multiple levels.

Once you have decided on the core reason or the 'why' of doing your business, you'll want to choose a visual representation that stands out and delivers your message in a way that potential customers will find hard to forget.

Develop a Logo

You are looking for a cleverly designed logo that drives your message. It should be simple while also providing a visual expression of your commitment. Logos can easily be simple and yet rich in meaning to represent some aspect of your company's mission.

Whether you choose to design the logo yourself or hire a graphic designer, take a moment to study some successful brands. This will help you to determine what style and flavor you are looking for in your logo. For example, if your focus is on eco-friendly soaps then you'll want to study popular organic brands and note the color choices, packaging materials, font choices and anything else they use that stands out when you look at them. Use your favorites from the list you make to develop your own design.

If you are on a budget like I was, try getting your design done for $5 from Fiverr.com. You can get almost anything designed or done at this site for just $5. But if you have little more to spare then try 99deisgns.com or some other freelance sites like

Freelancer.com, Guru.com or Upwork.com. You post a job description and get hundreds of designers to bid on your project, then hire the best candidate and get an awesome design done.

DESIGN RULES

No matter what type of logo you are going for, there are some basic guidelines and design rules you should keep in mind. There are a few things business owners have learned over the years that help with smart and effective logo design. By following these design rules, you can create a logo that will proudly and effectively represent your company for years to come.

Trendy elements may look good, but you don't want to push your design to the edge. Great design doesn't cost a lot, and neither does packaging, website design or marketing materials. A trendy design may look worn and dated in a few years. This will lead to the expense and loss of time to change the look of your logo. Rather focus on creating a logo today that will remain for years to come.

Always focus on your color palette. A logo needs to transfer nicely into a monotone for signage, packaging labels and marketing materials that are cheap and easy to print. If you have too many colors, it can also prevent you from using color psychology. Colors will evoke particular feelings. For example, bright yellows help entice a buyer by giving feelings of happiness and friendliness.

Lastly, pay attention to your fonts. There are a lot to choose from - script, curly, fun and eclectic. Avoid using anything too fancy. People don't want to spend time deciphering a font when they can read something at a glance and feel a connection. You also don't want to choose a standard font. You want to find a nice balance between easy to read and elegant. This will provide your logo with expression and interest.

Once you have a strong logo and tagline design, it is time to move on to other methods of making your brand stand out from the competition. Let's look at how you can develop a strong foundation for your brand and give yourself a leg up on the competition.

How to Make Your Brand Stand Out from the Competition

If you want to stand out from your competitors, you don't need a major investment or some grand plan. Rather you simply need to create a brand identity that people notice and remember. Consider four simple ways you can do this.

SET STANDARDS

Larger companies used brand guidelines in order to control the perception of the customer. They make sure that both online and offline customers are getting a consistent logo, marketing message, and experience no matter where they shop or what they purchase. As these aspects become predictable, potential customers will become more familiar with the brand. If this perception is positive then it will lead to trust and brand loyalty.

You can have the same unique and recognizable brand as well; even with a small business. Brand guidelines allow you an objective measure to make sure you consistently present your brand online and offline.

It will also simplify communication and expectations when outsourcing any business functions. While there will always be competition, what your customer perceives of your brand lasts forever. Consider the following when developing brand guidelines:

✧ What two or three fonts work with the logo?

✧ What color or color palettes work for my brand?

✧ What textures and materials help sell my brand message?

✧ What types of photos, scents, lighting, etc. help support my brand?

✧ What language style shows the essence of my brand?

EXPRESS YOURSELF

Everyone has a story to tell. Tell yours publicly and often till it becomes a point of differentiation for your company. You can tell your story on your website, on your blog, on social media, and in your product packaging. The key is to share your story in a compelling way while identifying product features and benefits. To do this, answer the following questions:

✧ Why did you start your business?
✧ What did you do before going into business for yourself?
✧ What is the inspiration behind your products?
✧ Why do you believe your products are better?
✧ Why did you choose your niche over others?

Tell your story not only in words; but also through photos, displays, and packaging.

Be Open to Customers

Everyone is creative on some level, but not everyone has the chances to be creative. You can stand out from the competition by educating your customers and helping them have a memorable, creative experience.

Put Customers First

While all businesses say customers come first, very few make the commitment through policies and procedures. Think about your business from the customer's point of view and see if there are any changes you can make. For example, can you make your return policy better than the competition? Do you make sure customers are 100% satisfied after a purchase?

Minor changes won't cost you a lot, but they can be the major difference in standing out from the competition. For the customer, it can be just the thing to come back again and recommend you to others. Of course, the only way to truly stand out and maintain your customers is to properly manage your brand.

Managing Your Brand

A lot of marketing experts will tell you that brand is everything, but what exactly does this mean for your liquid soap business? Knowing what this means is the key to your business's success in the future. Branding is about so much more than simply having a pretty logo and a strong statement. You need to learn how to manage your brand over time in order to be successful.

If you neglect your brand it can impact your growth and prevent you from gaining any business in the future. Mismanaging your brand will cause damage to your business that eventually causes people to go with your competition. To avoid this, let's look at how you can manage your brand.

THE PROMISE

Branding is all about getting your target market to trust you. This trust is what leads to purchases. From here it can develop into loyalty. The greatest brands are defined by their loyal customers. Therefore, when a customer buys your brand, the product needs to perform as you said it would so that you can fulfill your brand promise and gain the trust of your customers.

These people are more likely to become repeat customers. However, if you fail to meet customer expectations, then you can lose trust and potentially future business. Brand promises help you develop business statements and tell you where to focus your effort.

What promise do you offer? What specific need, desire or problem does your product routinely solve? Even if you don't know about a brand promise, you likely already have one. It is the reason your customers return and buy your products. If you don't know the reason behind a customer's purchase, then ask them so you can focus your marketing efforts and strengthen your brand. This will further increase your trust among customers since you can have strong marketing statements backed by strong product performance.

The best way to enforce your brand promise is through solid actions and clear messages. When you do this, you are creating a direct link between your products and the quality your customer continually expect from you.

When this link is disturb it will negatively impact your brand image. You also need to be careful of your personal behavior since this is also linked to trust and your brand. Even if marketing campaigns that aren't consistent with your brand may temporarily create an increase in sales or profits, this will have a negative impact on your business in the long run.

CONSISTENCY

You need to reinforce your brand promise over time with intentionality. This means that every action you take needs to be aligned with your brand promise. This includes marketing messages, campaigns, events, sponsorships, pricing strategy, discounting and everything you say. Any time you mismanage your product or position it wrong, you will be viewed as violating your brand promise by customers. Even product improvements can be mistaken by your customer base and viewed as a violation of your promise.

This doesn't mean you need to avoid improvements, but it just means you need to be careful when choosing what and how to make improvements. Once you make an improvement or change, you need to watch and listen to your customer's reactions carefully. Measure your results and be prepared to change back to the way things were if your brand is negatively impacted in the form of poor reviews or decreased sales.

Maintaining and managing your brand relies on consistency in all aspects of your products. Keep an eye on everything; monitor and protect every aspect of your brand every day. This includes both product quality and service. The longer you are able to maintain great customer service it will improve your reputation and become a valuable part of your brand promise. Any policy changes or lack of training that leads to poor experiences will break your consistency; eroding trust and damaging your brand.

Even making changes to your company name or logo may upset customers comfort level and have a negative impact on your brand. The name and image you choose for your brand is going to be imprinted on the minds and memories of your customers; it becomes familiar to them, and they learn to recognize it quickly. This is why it is important to carefully choose your names and images since you will be using it consistently and liberally for a long while. You should also develop a style guide, so you logo always appears consistent otherwise your customers will experience a disconnect of trust when they experience a variation in your product quality, packaging appearance, and customer service.

GROWING YOUR BRAND

Your brand is so much more than a logo. Your brand is the total experience your customers have with you. Your brand is everything. This encompasses your product quality, your customer service, your packaging and how your customers perceive your business.

When your customers have repeated positive experiences, you will earn loyalty and trust that helps build a thriving business. This is why you want to develop a brand promise and protect it through continual management and do everything you can to support it. Once you have a strong brand, the next thing you need to focus on is the proper pricing strategy of your products.

Pricing Your products

Before you set prices for your product, you want to consider seven things. It is easy to estimate the cost of supplies, but most neglect to account for the cost of things such as packaging and shipping. If you're going to have a successful small business, then you need to carefully consider your product pricing.

SYSTEMS

If you set up an accounting system, then much of the work is done for you. Most basic accounting software versions are affordable and get the job done for the most small businesses. The software will help by allowing you to instantly pull up a report and make sure your business is on track. Some of the top software on the market now are Freshbooks, Quickbooks, and Xero. Here is a link to a review from PC Magazine on top 10 accounting and bookkeeping software.

http://www.pcmag.com/article2/

COST OF GOODS SOLD

You want to do this for each product. Calculate cost not only for using a total box or bottle but for partial supply use as well. After breaking down ingredient costs for a single batch of soap then divide it by what the batch produces to get your costs of goods for raw materials. However, this is only the first step.

PACKAGING AND SHIPPING

Make sure you do the same process to account for the packaging and shipping per container of soap.

HUMAN CAPITAL

Whether you intend to or not, human capital is something you must address. At some point, you may need to hire additional people and not considering human capital can result in failure. Consider what your baseline wage will be depending on your location. Increase the hourly rate by 10-25% to account for the cost of time and payroll as well as the cost of benefits. At the end, divide how much each employee is paid per batch by the number of containers to include with your cost-per-container.

OPERATIONS

Next, you need to consider facility and operations costs. Even if you are working from home, there will still be costs to consider in this area. Think about space and utilities. Plus, if your business grows you may one day move to a location with more production space. Also, don't forget to add the cost of liability insurance. It is best to calculate 10% to cover these expenses unless you already have a facility and know specific costs.

MARKETING AND SALES

There is the old saying: *You have to spend money to make money*. Consider the following potential expenses when operating your business:

✓ Website maintenance

✓ Business cards

- ✓ Networking events
- ✓ Social media
- ✓ Travel
- ✓ Mileage
- ✓ Trade association membership
- ✓ Booth fees
- ✓ Donations
- ✓ Packaging
- ✓ Advertising
- ✓ Credit card processing fees

It is best to track how much time you spend on marketing and assign it an amount, such as $20 an hour. This will often add 5-10% to per unit cost depending on how much you sell.

Now that you've finished calculations you can focus on pricing your product. Take your calculated total unit price and double it to get your lowest wholesale per container price. Allow some room for incentives or special pricing in the event of new accounts or special situations. Round up to get your pricing. However, there is still an important factor in how high you can charge. If your total unit cost is $2 than your wholesale unit cost should be roughly at $4.

Your final price is largely determined by branding. Consider who your target market is and whether that makes you a luxury, mid or bargain brand. The most important thing is that you don't price lower than the competition for the sake of competing. If needed you can offer incentives or sales to lower your price.

Lastly, keep the following tips in mind when pricing your brand/product:

❖ Have enough storage to buy products in bulk for lower prices.

- ❖ Always have a backup supplier in place should your initial supplier run out of supplies.

- ❖ Order in advance, so you don't have to pay for express shipping.

- ❖ Set an annual budget and allow room for increased supply cost, improvement and updated costs, and marketing costs.

- ❖ Update your pricing as needed to cover increased expenses.

- ❖ Always remember to include some pay for yourself.

Now that you've determined the per unit price of your liquid soaps you can start focusing on marketing and advertising methods. Let's consider your options for promoting your business.

How to Promote & Grow Your Business

Most small business owners will tell you that the best form of advertising is word-of-mouth, and it is one of the cheapest options for business promotion. However, there are lots of other ways to promote your business both online and offline. Next, I'll consider some of the creative ways that you may be able to promote your liquid soap business and find new customers but before we do, let me mention a great marketing book that inspired me and motivated me to think out the box.

The book is "Sales Genie - Retail Marketing 101" Even though this book isn't meant for soap business, rather the author focused mostly on retail convenience store type retail operations. But the ideas, strategies, tips and tricks he shared were so very unconventional(at least to me) that I got very inspired by it. I can honestly say that I took a lot of his ideas and implemented in my business and saw success. I highly recommend this book to anyone for out of the box marketing, and sales boost ideas.

NEWSLETTERS

This option can work both online and offline. At one time it was an entirely offline method for promoting a business. The offline option can get quite expensive with the costs of printing and postage. However, online monthly newsletters are now basically free and just require your time. Use the email addresses you get from your website to electronically send out regular newsletters to keep your loyal customers informed of new products and services along with sales and special deals.

LOYALTY PROGRAMS

Airlines use frequent flyer programs as the main attraction for a long time now. A lot of restaurants and other retail stores are starting to follow the same or similar type of reward models. As a small business, you too can do something similar to attract customers. Consider giving discounts to customers who pay above a certain amount in a complete purchase. You can easily design a loyalty program that is unique to your business and keeps your customers coming back to you for more.

NETWORKING

There are plenty of groups, plus the Chamber of Commerce that can put you in contact with others in the local small business community. Not only will you be able to engage with people who know what it is like running a small business, but you will also be able to showcase your commitment to growth and the local community. Posting this membership in your marketing campaigns will certainly go a long way towards creating a favorable and positive image.

VIDEOS

Consider putting together an eye-catching video that promotes your business. There is no better way to promote your products and services that with a compelling video. You can place the video on your website in a prominent spot where it will get maximum views. Search engines also do well with videos along with YouTube, so you will be able to take advantage of multiple communication channels when distributing your message and promoting your products.

CONTESTS AND AWARDS

Create a few unique contests worthwhile for the customers to enter. Also, make sure you vary the theme and awards to continually encourage participation. Some options include free products, discounts, gift cards and other types of sweepstakes. Publicize your contests and find creative ways to make them public as well as officially recognizing the winners.

WORK WITH OTHERS

Take the time to find a company that sells products which compliment your own, but doesn't directly compete with you. Approach them about an exclusive marketing deal in which you work together. Then you can each showcase the others work without much effort or money involved.

Today's digital society has opened a whole new set of options for business advertising. Social media now plays a huge role in marketing strategies, but social media isn't a true advertising method unless you buy ads on one of its platforms. If you want to have a presence online, then you need to consider some of the following online advertising options when developing a marketing strategy.

ONLINE PRESENCE

The key to a strong online presence all starts with having a professional website. Any advertising you do online and offline needs to point potential customers to your website. A lot of business now buy ads that display a website first, rather than the address or telephone number that used to be common not long ago. Often a customer that contacts you through your website is going to be more serious than an individual that just responds to a random ad. Your website needs to stay fresh and updated. A good option is to consider writing a blog to keep traffic coming to your site. Another option is to make sure you reserve a page on your site for customer testimonials.

SOCIAL MEDIA

I put social media first because lately, this is the most powerful and most effective way to promote your business. If you already have a strong social media presence, you should use that to your advantage.

Out of all the avenues of social media, for this niche, the best mediums are Facebook, Instagram, and Pinterest. But Facebook is by far the best when connecting with friends and family and reaching out their friends and family and before you know it, the reach can grow into thousands of customers and all for free.

SEARCH ENGINES

At one time you would have looked into listing your business in the yellow pages, but now most people do their searches online. For this reason, you want to focus on getting your business and website listed in online directories and search engines. Some options to consider are the following:

- ➤ Google Places
- ➤ Yahoo!
- ➤ Yelp
- ➤ Bing
- ➤ CitySearch
- ➤ LinkedIn
- ➤ YellowPages.com
- ➤ Foursquare
- ➤ MapQuest
- ➤ Angie's List
- ➤ Yellow Book

SEO Marketing

SEO or Search Engine Optimization is the way to optimize your website in order to attract generic search traffic. SEO techniques can allow a well-constructed website to attract visitors without the need for paid advertising. Utilizing SEO techniques can help you to get to the top of free search links. If you don't have the ability to do this yourself, you can hire someone to help with SEO optimization. If you want to try it yourself consider the follow SEO optimization tips:

❖ Keep your website simple and easy to navigate.

❖ Have a site map.

❖ Have a list of top keywords to use in URLs, page content, website title tags and page headers.

❖ Have internal links that target specific pages and link other relevant sites back to yours.

❖ Have a referrer log for your site so you can determine the effectiveness of search terms.

❖ Routinely monitor your results through services such as Google Toolbar and Alexa to know where your site clicks are coming from.

ONLINE ADS (PPC)

Although with SEO strategies, a lot of businesses choose to buy ads through services such as Google AdWords. Basically, you pay for an ad anytime someone clicks on them, and you control how much you pay per click. The higher the click rates for your website, the closer to the top of the page you'll get where you're more likely to get seen.

You are allowed to set a daily budget that won't be exceeded, and you can even control the area where the ad is seen so you won't have to worry about attracting customers from areas you can't service. It is important to come up with a list of keywords the people are likely to search for since this is what will trigger the appearance of your ad.

PITCH YOUR COMPANY

When you run a small business, marketing becomes an ongoing process. This means you need to be prepared to pitch your company at any time. It may be during a phone call, a surprise visitor or just a random encounter. You need to be always prepared to promote your company.

This means you need to grab a person's attention without stumbling for the right promotional words. Make sure you come up with a compelling pitch that summarizes your business and products within a few minutes or less. If you can't capture people's attention in this amount of time then you may lose a potential sale.

TRADITIONAL MEDIA

While this internet is becoming a popular place to advertise a business, it still relies on customers to come to you. This is where traditional advertising is still popular since it puts your message direction in front of an audience through means such as cable television, radio, and newspapers. These advertising methods are more expensive, but you can target specific geographic areas and demographics to reduce the total cost involved. Local media can be beneficial when you're first getting started.

PLASTER YOUR LOGO

You should never miss an opportunity to market your business logo and message. Place your business logo on anything connected with your company. Also try to make yourself visible to the community by sponsoring local sports teams, doing public speaking, distributing fliers and other forms of local advertising. You can supplement these tactics by using social media as well.

As you can tell, there are plenty of advertising methods. However, all of this advertising won't do you any good if you don't know how to turn it into sales. So next let's consider the process of making sales and how you can master the art.

The Art of Sales

When you're first starting out with your liquid soap business, you probably won't have a large budget for marketing. As a result, you are going to need to rely on hard work, creativity and meeting customer needs in order to have success. You can do this by providing customers with a buying experience that a larger business can't. This is accomplished through four things:

1. Unique products
2. Super high quality
3. Exceptional service
4. Guaranteed satisfaction

As a small business owner, you also have the advantage of offering personal service and developing a lasting relationship with customers. There is nothing more valuable to a small business than gaining customers who trust you. This should be your main goal. To do this consider the following.

TAKE A PERSONAL INTEREST

Customers sometimes prefer to do business with a small operation because they want personal attention. While this places a greater challenge on the small business owner, it can also be an advantage that should be embraced. You will be able to demonstrate your products while offering advice and recommendations directly to interested customers.

When you have the opportunity to get to know your customers on a personal level, you can suggest products that are of interest to them. This places you in a unique position to close sales that come from other promotional methods. When you use your personal relationships with customers, you will be able to solidify your brand and develop loyalty.

KNOWLEDGE

This is often the foundation of the art of sales. Consider the last time you purchased something you didn't know a lot about and how the salesperson helped you with their knowledge. Product knowledge brings together the benefits and features of products. Customers purchase based on benefits first and features second. If you know what a customer wants and needs then you can adequately describe a product to them. Some common benefits include the following:

> Convenience
> Pleasure
> Safety
> Time-saving
> Utility
> Appearance

➤ Artistic value

This reasons are sometimes intangible but are what motivate people to purchase your products. The features are tangible aspects of your products that make them stand out from the competition. Features are very important, but you also need to emphasize how they can benefit the individual.

POTENTIAL CUSTOMERS

When you come into contact with potential new customers, first impressions and timing are everything. You want a potential customer to feel welcome and comfortable. This is a little more challenging if most of your sales are online, but you will use the same tactics online that you do for any other communication method.

If a customer isn't interested after the initial contact, it will be difficult to recover. Customers want an environment of trust and a sense that you'll go the extra mile to maximize their shopping experience. While caring for customers seems obvious, you shouldn't take it for granted. People will know within a minute or less if you are sincere in your desire to help. Show customers you care by your words and then back it up with actions.

There are a number of ways that you can engage new customers based on your circumstances. You can start up a friendly conversation, provide additional information about your products or encourage customer questions. No matter what, you should be prompt and courteous without making customers feel like you're trying to make a sale.

It is also important to rely on social media and feedback from loyal customers to keep up to date on customer tastes, trends, and preferences. You can stay ahead of the competition by adapting to changing trends and customer needs. Whenever you offer a new product, special discount or other promotional event, then you should make it known to everyone.

Help Them Make a Decision

Today, customers are faced with more choices than ever before. The internet has drastically changed the way people shop and gather information. You can use this trend to your advantage. Create a website that contains a lot of images and information about liquid soap and its related products.

To turn a potential customer into a purchasing customer, you need to convince them that they are balancing perceived value with out-of-pocket cost. You can do this through advice and additional product information.

After a purchase is made, ask questions like what motivated the purchase. Customers often want information that shows a product is meeting their needs and that the products you are offering are the best solution to meeting that need. As a small business owner, you are in the perfect position to reinforce a customer's need and reassure them that your products are well worth their money.

COMPLETING THE SALE

Liquid soap products should sell themselves, but it isn't something you should rely on as a small business owner. After all, your products aren't in front of potential customers every day. Therefore, completing a sale will depend on the individual customer. However, by this point in a transaction you should know the customer you are dealing with and what will motivate them to make a purchase. At this point, you should remind individuals of the benefits and why you feel your product meets their needs.

When closing a sale, you want to emphasize the advantages of buying new rather than waiting until later. Do this through recent objective testimonials. Now would be the time to offer special incentives like discounts or credits towards other purchases. If you are confident you can close a sale, then your customer will sense it. This is more effective than pressuring someone with sales techniques.

You also want to keep an eye on the customer. Look at their body language and reactions. Also, make sure you listen carefully to their comments and questions. This will give you all the necessary information to close a sale.

Once you've learned how to make a sale, it is important to consider the second most important art that of making the up-sell.

Helpful Tips to Up-Sell

The most important thing for a small business owner is to improve order value and potential profitability. How do you do this? You need to sell up. Consider the following tips to help you up-sell.

THINK STRATEGY

The key to upselling is knowing what products and services add value based on a customer's specific purchases. Upselling is effective when it incorporates offers as a natural extension of the customer's basic need. Customers are more likely to take advantage of an upsell when it is a related product.

TIME IT RIGHT

Up-selling is often more successful when approached as a casual afterthought than a hard sell. Timing is the key in this. Customers are more likely to respond positively to upsell once they know for sure that they'll buy something.

CORRECT PRICING

A customer is more likely to up-sell if your price and packaging allow them to instantly recognize added value without going too much over the cost of their intended purchase. You need to make sure up-sells are an easy decision. The goal of the up-sell is to improve average order value without being too aggressive in pricing. You shouldn't ask a customer to pay any more than 20% of their initial purchase.

USE THE SEASONS

Some of your best opportunities for up selling are during special events and seasonal occasions. You can do this through craft shows, email, and online promotions. For example, during the holidays you can make smaller versions of your top selling products and offer them at a reduced price. A seasonal up sell does best when it solves a customer's problem since they'll be more likely to make an impulse purchase.

LOCATION IS EVERYTHING

An up sell needs to seem more like a customer's idea than yours. Try merchandising up-sell items near a checkout counter at craft shows and other retail locations. You can also present them as a suggested item during checkout on your e-commerce site. These up-sell items should quickly show their use, value, and benefit.

In a retail environment, this means showing samples that can be handled. Online you'll need to showcase up-sell products with their complimenting products. The price should be clearly marked so the customer can quickly add it to their purchase.

Now that you know how to make a sale and upsell to add revenue; it is also important to know how you can increase sales. There are seven ways to do this.

7 Ways to Increase Sales

Simply working on marketing and sales aren't the only ways to increase sales. Often your existing customers and prospect list is all you need to increase sales. Consider the following tips to help you expand your offerings, grow your market and increase visibility.

UP SELL

As we've already discussed in the art of up-selling; this option entices customers to make additional purchases of a more expensive product. Even if a small percentage of customers make the upgrade, it can still be enough to double or even triple your income.

CROSS SELL

When a client makes a purchase, think about something else they need or want. Ask yourself if there is a new line of related soap products that you can offer a customer at a point of sale. If you are selling through a website, set up your shopping cart program to offer suggested companions at checkout. You'll be surprised at how fast impulse purchases add up and increase your revenue.

WORK WITH OTHERS FOR REFERENCES

Are there other products or services a client may need that you don't provide? Can you refer out to other businesses for a profit split or a fee-for-referral basis? Perhaps you have a local community where you can have an information relationship with networked businesses that help generate business together and serve clients. This will help build relationships both with the customer and with other business owners as well.

ANALYZE MISSED SALES

Often once businesses hear no, they never look back at the prospect. However, statistics shows that nearly 40% of customers who make purchases have said no at one time or another. Rather consider these prospects and what you can offer them to get a sale. Is there an up sell or incentive that you can offer to encourage a purchase. On the other hand, you can simply continue to tell them about your business until they eventually make a purchase. The best way to do this is through mailing lists.

CONSIDER STALE LEADS

All businesses have several leads that have faded over time. Contact these leads and entice them into becoming purchasing customers. Do this through sales, special gift offers and new products. All of these can bring people back and convert them into paying customers. You spent a lot of time and effort getting people to know about your business, and you shouldn't just give up on them.

USE INPUT

Find ways to get feedback and ideas from customers and prospects. Offer to let them beta test new products for a reduce price or even free. The feedback and buzz will help your business. You can also use social media to keep customers and prospects abreast of new developments. Offer voting, surveys, and other feedback options. This will also help make new customers aware of your great customer service policies.

Testimonials

A single good testimonial is the same as about a dozen advertising campaigns. Don't be afraid to ask clients to share how a product benefited them. These stories can help increase sales and make new customers. There are plenty of people who are willing to talk about products they like, you simply need to ask or offer an avenue for them. Ask them to fill out a questionnaire or upload to your Facebook page. If you make it easy for a person, they will do it and it can attract new customers or additional sales.

However, this is just dealing with sales in general. As a new small business owner the majority of your liquid soap sales are going to come from local markets and craft fairs. It is important to know how you can improve your sales at these events since it will be the majority of your income until you grow your business.

Grow Your Sales in Marketplace

Selling at various local markets accounts for the bulk of sales for small businesses and also builds your reputation within the local community. However, each market and craft fair presents a different venue that requires a unique strategy than you would use online or in a retail setting. Consider the following ways that you can make your presence at a market a success.

RESEARCH

Each market is going to vary in demographics, culture and rules and regulations. There are some markets that only allow known or branded products while others are open to any homemade goods. Other venues have geographic requirements. Even with two markets that are open to the same people, they will have different participation and attendance guidelines. You need to do your research and contact that market manager at least a year in advance to learn about demographics as well as the rules and regulations involved.

TEST

After you've done your research, don't jump into tents and displays. Rather you want to test the markets and choose ones that offer the best benefit. It is a good idea to go for markets that allow you to sell as a daily vendor. It is always better to approach a market slowly rather than simply jumping in a finding out the consequences later.

STRATEGIZE

The color is crucial when selling at a booth. In fact, statistics shows that colors account for 85% of sales at markets. For example, yellow is a happy and optimistic color that inspires customers to take action. On the other hand, green is a color linked with purity and naturalness. Take the time to research colors that bring out the reaction you want in customers. Then consider the best setup for your booth that will attract customers. Avoid signage with scripted fonts and busy backgrounds; rather you want to focus on simple and easy to read designs that are consistent.

ORGANIZATION AND PRACTICE

Selling at markets is going to test your organizational skills. You have a limited window of time to set up and break down your booth. If you aren't prepared the day can go badly. Make sure you are organized by packing your gear and supplies in clearly marked and numbered containers. Focus on packing them into your vehicle in a way that makes it easy to set up your booth.

Before the big day, take the time to do some practice runs. There is a lot that goes into selling at a market: loading the marketing materials and goods, traveling, parking, unloading, setting up and then breaking down at the end of the day. All of this takes time and energy.

Drive to the market a few times before the big days to make sure you don't face unexpected delays such as construction. Keep a checklist on hand, so you don't forget important items. Practice how long it will take to realistically set up and be ready for customers.

CONSIDER THE AUDIENCE

To maximize potential at a market, you need to focus on the details. Ask the market organizer to tell you about the audience and how best to serve them through logistics, operations and price points. If you know other vendors selling at the market, ask for personal experiences. If possible, consider walking around the market before you setup your own booth.

You can use the feedback you get to help develop a customer experience strategy that meets all of a customer's needs.

PAYMENT METHODS

It is important to have multiple methods of payment. Be aware that fewer people are carrying cash. Even if there are credit card fees involved, these are part of doing business and can be reflected in your pricing; plus they are tax deductible for you. In addition, make sure you bring plenty of change. Customers don't like being asked for smaller bills. The goal is to make it easy for people to make a payment and purchase your products.

Accepting credit cards as a small vendor has become easier with all the new technology, and there are many companies that provide these services. Most times all you need a small credit card scanner attached or connected to your mobile phone, and you are in business. I started out with a company call Square. You can look them up at www.squareup.com

AVOID DISCOUNTS

A lot of market vendors tend to offer discounts at the end-of-the-day since they don't want to pack up their products or they think it will make the market more profitable. If this were the case, then everyone would wait until the last minute to shop; thereby decreasing profits for everyone. Using this strategy will also minimize the value of your product for potential new customers.

TAKE PICTURES

It is important to build up an online audience that helps promote market outings. Pinterest, Instagram, Facebook, and Twitter are all valuable sources. A good booth display will also give you an advantage on social media since the images posted account for 87% of all interaction. In comparison, posts without images only get about 4% interaction. If you can't post during the day while at a market, it is okay to do it at the end of the day.

You can even use the images to invite people to the next market.

PREPARE YOURSELF

Preparing for a weekend flea market can be difficult in adjusting your sleep pattern alone, but it can be even harder if you have a full-time job as well. You don't want to be exhausted when going to a market since this can negatively impact sales.

So make sure you have a good breakfast and healthy snacks to get you through the day. Have good shoes if you're going to be on your feet all day. Have everything you need to be prepared to make it through the whole day.

DEVELOP RELATIONSHIPS

Markets often have a high customer return rate, so you need to engage customers and build a relationship. Ask questions and don't try to talk too much about yourself. However, give plenty of information on your product and how you make it.

Building a strong relationship will lead to long-term customers who return for additional purchases.

DOCUMENT EVERYTHING

You may think you'll remember everything, but you probably won't. You are going to meet a lot of people at a market, and all of them will have differing opinions. If you get asked the same product related question more than once; make a note of it. If people pay more attention to one product than another, note that as well. All of these notations will help with marketing research and will help direct your product development and marketing strategy in the future. It can help you learn what the customer wants.

However, just because you make a good majority of your income from markets doesn't mean you should neglect other avenues as well. Consider how you can sell to small retailers.

Selling to Local Retailers

When it comes time to expand your liquid soap business beyond local markets, it can be a good idea to consider expanding to small retail stores. The key to marketing to these stores is planning and research. Let's look at how you can be successful.

Before approaching retailers of any size, you first need proof of concept. This is gained through a solid history of sales in both local and online. A smaller boutique or retail store is the perfect place to gain experience and learn before moving on to larger retailers. You need to provide proof that you can fulfill orders on time and that you have adequate inventory.

Next, you want to focus on a quality sell sheet. This is a one-page brochure that highlights all the facts about your business and products. You will leave this brochure with retailers you visit, so you need to make sure it properly reflects your brand. Sometimes it can be a good idea to hire a professional designer if you aren't comfortable doing it yourself. You can get flyers, brochure, business cards and even your logo and product labels designed at same sites I mentioned earlier, like Fiverr.com, 99designs.com and few other freelancer sites I mentioned before.

The important things to include are the following:

✧ High-quality images of your products and in-store displays.

✧ Simple ordering information.

✧ MSRP price. Don't offer a price sheet up front. Your costs to sell will vary between retailers, and you can never raise your price.

✧ Partner and customer testimonials after you've sold at a location for a while.

✧ Emphasize uniqueness if you have trademarked or patented products. Tell why retailers should buy your product and what makes you different from the competition.

✧ Provide any social proof if you have it; including awards, seals of approval, endorsements or any media attention.

✧ Contact information including email, phone, and website.

It is always best to visit a small retailer in person. They are often too busy to return calls. If you stop in person, they will often take a few moments to speak with you. It is also beneficial to have a personal connection. Show your personal side and express interest in the shop and owner.

Small retailers are in the same position as you, they need strong margins and help with marketing. Show the owners you are willing to assist with marketing. Offer things such as specials, cost-saving measures and in-store product demos for customers. Also, offer to teach your product line to sales personnel. Having a strong social media presence can also allow you to promote stores that are carrying your products and share their ads.

Small retailers often struggle to compete with larger retailers when it comes to pricing. As a result, most small retailers turn to unique and high-quality products for a competitive advantage. You can help with this by offering stunning packaging and displays, favorable terms with high margins, a simple ordering process and excellent customer service. Avoid displays that take up a lot of room, glitchy ordering systems or being overly talkative.

This may seem like a lot of work, and it will require effort on your part, but it will also offer a lot of benefits and rewards. So take the time to focus on small retailers and boutiques first before going to larger retailers. The last area of sales that you want to focus on is online.

E-Commerce

All businesses seem to have a website these days. Even retailers that have long had a store presence are developing an online presence. If you are just getting started as a small business then having an online presence is the fastest, easiest and cheapest way to get a product niche going.

Let's consider the basics of e-commerce and what you need to have an internet presence for your small business. E-commerce is often driven by software, so you may need to talk with an expert when determining what is best for your business. Spending a little money on experts up front will often save you time and money later.

A STRONG WEBSITE

The most important part of e-commerce is to have a strong website. Your website is going to be the first thing potential customers see. A website should be easy to navigate and professional in appearance. However, for you; what is happening behind the scenes is just as important. It is important that you have a company hosting your website with the appropriate server capacity to perform all of the functions of an online store.

In addition, you want to consider website factors such as reliability, technical support, bandwidth and special features. As your business grows; you want to know that your site will continue to function and handle customers. When your site goes offline, it is the same as locking your business doors.

Nowadays it has become very easy to open an online store without hiring a team of programmers and developers and spend thousands of dollars. There are companies are like Shopify, Wix, Square Space and may others. These companies made it very simple for anyone without programming knowledge to open and populate an e-commerce store with ease. They provide a full storefront for you including the shopping cart and even online payment processing options. Often if you can find a good promotional coupon from one of those e-store builders, you can open an online store for less than $100 per month

Here is a comparison chart of the top 5 E-commerce store builders, take a look.

http://www.websitebuilderexpert.com/e-commerce-online-store-builders-comparison-chart/

ONLINE CATALOGS

When you are trying to sell online, first impressions are everything. If a customer isn't happy with the website, you won't have a chance to convince them to stay. Customers will quickly move on to the next website. Therefore, a good online catalog will quickly grab a customer's attention and hold it. For potential customers, perception is key if they aren't familiar with your products. The way your catalog is designed and how you present your products has a great impact on turning people into buyers.

You online catalog needs to have all the information needed for customers to make a decision; this should include the following at a minimum:

- ✓ Specifications
- ✓ Sizes
- ✓ Colors
- ✓ Materials
- ✓ Warranty
- ✓ Weight

If you can't answer all of a potential customers questions within the product description, then you may lose a sale since a customer won't take the time to ask questions; they'll simply move on to another site. You want to take the time to develop a top quality catalog, but it will be worth the effort. The catalog needs to be kept current and attractive. The customer needs to be able to easily sort and compare products.

INTERFACE

The interface is just as important as the website itself. The interface is the tool used to control and update your store. It combines all of the functions needed to operate and maintain your store, including the important shopping cart. An interface should be flexible and robust while also being easy to use. The interface needs to allow you to expand and enhance your website as your business grows. Choosing a host that provides you with the tools and capacity to perform complex tasks easily is the best option.

THE SHOPPING CART

After a customer decides to buy an item, your shopping cart should be straightforward and foolproof. This is where an order is confirmed and payments processed, so don't give people any reason to not complete a purchase. Before a customer gives you payment information, they want to know the price that includes taxes, shipping, and handling. The checkout process should show all of this on the first screen. If a customer doesn't see this until the last screen, they may back out of a purchase.

You also need to make sure you are only asking for just enough personal information to complete the purchase. Clearly show how the item is going to be shipped and have an estimated shipping time after the destination address is known. Offer as many payment methods as possible in order to improve customer convenience.

WEBSITE SECURITY

In today's technological society, security is a major concern for customers. There are stories in the news every day about hackers getting personal information from major retailers. Before they give you their credit card information, customers want to know they are protected.

For an online business, the first thing you need to answer is whether you'll store payment information on the website or redirect it to a PCI-compliant gateway merchant that processes online payments. For a small business, the latter is often the best and least expensive option.

In addition to payment processing, there are a lot of others aspects that can't be covered in this simple article. It is best to talk with a hosting company or an independent expert in order to make sure your website has all of the security measures needed to protect customer's personal information.

SHIPPING OPTIONS

For some online shoppers, the cost of shipping is enough to turn them away from a sale. This is especially true with expensive purchases. A lot of businesses get rid of this problem by offering reduced or free shipping after a minimum purchase amount. This policy has proven very successful for business such as Amazon. The most common option is to provide different shipping options with various delivery speeds and costs. It is important that customers know the total cost before they place their order.

A customer based website is important to attracting new customers and converting them into sales. Prompt and effective service is the key before, during and after purchases to keep customers coming back again. Have clear policies about warranties, returns, and exchanges. Once you have successfully set up a variety of sales avenues and learned how to make sales, you need to maintain them. The first step is using data to keep top customers.

Keeping Track of Customers and Keeping Them Happy

The statistics show that three-quarters of small business sales come from one-quarter of customers. This means it is very important that you hold onto top customers. The key to success is to understand spending habits. When developing marketing strategies, promotional campaigns and expansion plans; you want to keep top customers in mind and center your focus on them.

This doesn't mean you won't spend time trying to find new customers. It means you shouldn't take top customers for granted and just assume they'll stick with your products. Take the time to identify your top customers and the opportunities they present; then develop relationships with them that keep them coming back. The process isn't that simple, but it is well worth the effort.

DATA COLLECTION

Thanks to a number of computer programs, data collection is a fairly simple process. For this reason you should fully maximize your benefits of data collection. The primary reason for data collection is to get the best targeted marketing. For data collection to be successful you need to gather the following:

➢ Customer name, address and contact info so you can have direct, personalized communication during any needed follow-ups.

➢ Personal details of customers including gender, age, birth date, income, and employment; this will help give you a picture of your most typical customer.

➢ Get to know your customer's interests such as hobbies, sports, and their free time activities. This allows you to focus marketing campaigns and develop opportunities to cater to customers interests.

➢ Keep a history of customer purchases. This not only includes the products they purchase, but also their frequency, timing and dollar value. Understanding the spending habits allows you to categorize customers as impulse buyers, comparative shoppers, considered purchasers or regular customers. This helps with both pricing development and promotional tactics.

➢ Also, consider payment history. Know the primary method of payment customers use and how likely they are to pay on time.

➢ Lastly, keep track of customer communications. Track all responses to outgoing communications and use it to maximize the timing and effectiveness of future communications.

HOW TO COLLECT DATA

Due to privacy concerns, some of this information is difficult to get, but you should get as much as possible without harassing. Larger companies will hire market research firms, but you can do the same with an online database to catalog data. Just make sure the method of data collection you use meets all federal, state and local laws on data collection and storage. Some ways you can do this include the following:

Orders

Customers often don't want to give up any more information than what's necessary for a transaction. You can set up "optional" sections and explain to customers that you'll only use it to personalize products and services. You can also encourage people to register at your website, so they don't have to keep re-entering their information. Mutual trust will build in time, and your collection efforts will grow.

Surveys

Many customers are wary of this form of information gathering. People routinely send out surveys that end up asking for donations. If you are going to do surveys, you should make them genuine and directly connected to your business.

Offer to send the results to all participants and then maintain your promise.

Competitions

Periodically consider having a contest with prizes. During the sign-up process, customers will often give information. However, you shouldn't ask for more than a name, email address and zip code to avoid scaring people away. You can always ask for more information later.

Research

You can often find some current market research data that gives you information on demographic patterns and emerging trends. While this research won't be unique to your business, they will help provide statistics that help determine business conditions and forecasts.

DATA ANALYSIS

You need to understand the dynamics of your existing customer base to influence customer behavior. The data you gather can allow you to isolate personal and shopping traits of your top clients. Using this information you can design pricing strategies and marketing tactics that attract and reward customers within the demographic. Develop communication programs that entice customers to return and encourage loyal customers to spend more. The database can also allow you to target certain products and prices at the right time of the year.

CONNECT WITH OTHERS

Find online forums related to liquid soap and then offer free products to genuinely interested people. Answer questions, but don't make people feel pressured to purchase your products. Allow your website to speak for itself and word will spread through social media. Also, encourage feedback through your site and go over it regularly. Personally responding to comments will impress potential customers. Offer website visitors the option of signing up for email bulletins/newsletter, but always offer a way to opt-out of communications. Mailchimp.com is a great free resource if you want to send out monthly newsletters to your customers.

It doesn't take a lot of money to make customers feel special. Use email or text to set up automated birthday notes. Adding a simple personal touch such as this will really improve overall customer experience. The goal is to keep customers who generate profit and revenue. You create highly satisfied customers when you aren't overbearing and intrusive. To do this, put yourself in the customer's shoes and avoid things that would offend you. Also, make sure you use common sense.

However, this doesn't mean you simply focus all your time and effort on the top customers. You still want to keep all customers happy, so they return to make future purchases. Let's look at some ways to keep your customers happy.

Keeping Customers Happy

Without customers, you wouldn't have a business very long. Sometimes it can be a subtle and trivial thing that turns a customer away from returning to you. Attracting customers cost money, and once you gain a happy customer, you don't want to lose them. Statistics have shown that it costs five times more to find a new customer than it does to keep a satisfied customer. While some turnover is unavoidable, doing a few simple things can improve customer loyalty and can lead to return customer that help to maximize your profits.

FIRST IMPRESSION IS THE KEY

From the moment you meet someone they will form an impression of you and determine if they ever want to meet you again. This first impression is critical in the business world because a paying customer is on the line. These first impressions are like a lifeline for your small business.

You need to ask yourself what makes a good first impression. The answer lies in the entire interaction from beginning to end. It encompasses everything the customer sees, hears, touches smells or tastes during the first encounter. Since there is so much depending on these first impressions, you want to have a positive, successful image. It is extremely difficult to overcome a negative first impression. It can also lead to harmful word-of-mouth publicity that can have an even bigger impact.

To create a last first impression you definitely want to do the following:

❖ Look professional when meeting potential customers.

❖ When talking about your products, speak with authority and credibility.

❖ Get to the point when answering questions and do so objectively.

❖ Your workspace should be safe, clean, attractive, organized and professional.

- ❖ If you have employees, train them in customer service and relations.
- ❖ Maintain an adequate and current inventory of products.
- ❖ Make transactions straightforward and smooth.

The key to a successful business is to have a lasting and positive first impression. There is a lot of competition in the liquid soap business, so you can't afford any mistakes. Establish your credibility, and you will soon find word spreading, giving you a form of advertising you can't purchase.

There are also plenty of common sense steps you can take to promote and develop customer loyalty, so they return. Most of these steps don't cost you a thing and only require a few seconds. Be sure to remember the following:

- ❖ Don't take new or regular customers for granted.

- ❖ Make customers understand that the heart of your business goals involve their best interests.

- ❖ Openly tell customers how important they are for you and your business.

- ❖ Encourage customers to return for future purchases.

- ❖ Learn enough about customers to tailor individual service to them.

- ❖ Encourage customer contact when you think the business can provide a unique solution to their problem.

- ❖ Follow up with customers to make sure the order was filled properly and on time.

- ❖ Handle any complaints or problems quickly and efficiently.

- ❖ Make sure any corrective action is satisfactory to the customer.

Managing Complaints

It is important that you listen to customers and encourage them to provide you with feedback. Customers are an excellent source to use as business consultants since they are not only cheaper, but they'll also tell you both the positives and negatives. Record feedback from customers and consider devoting a section of your website specifically for this purpose.

If you receive a complaint, respond to it genuinely and empathize with the specific problem. Ask questions to help you fully understand the scope of the issue and ask the individual to suggest solutions that can help get a successful resolution to the issue. View the complaint as constructive criticism and use it to make permanent improvements to your business.

Customers expect business owners to act responsibly and quickly, even if it requires time and money. Have a personal response ready that matches with your procedures and policies. Act quickly when you receive a complaint and maintain a log that shows not only the complaint but the proposed solution and the date of the action. If a resolution isn't achieved right away, keep the customer informed of any progress until the issue is solved. Then make sure you follow up with the customer to make sure they are happy with the outcome.

Customers will take note of business owners who are fair and equitable in dealing with complaints, even if they don't get entirely what they want. Treat your customers with respect and do what you can to understand them; this will be appreciated, and you'll often be rewarded with a loyal customer.

CUSTOMER LOYALTY PROGRAMS

A lot of businesses, large and small, offer reward programs as incentives to choose them over other companies. These programs exist for a reason, they work. You can do the same thing, just on a smaller scale. Think of a reward program that is unique to your business. This can be as simple as offering a discount when customers reach a certain amount. Make customers aware of your program and make it easy to sign up for.

When you run a small business, some level of customer loss is going to happen and is unavoidable. The best you can hope to do is minimize the loss and keep improving your ability to reach max customer satisfaction.

The internet has drastically changed the marketing scene, and many businesses can find new and cheap ways to promote themselves. It also means customers have the chance to review products they purchased in real-time. Vendors who sell on sites such as eBay and Amazon need to rely on reviews while other businesses rely on reviews on sites such as Yelp.

Now that we've looked at all the aspects of starting and maintaining your business, it is a good idea to finish up by taking a moment to look at how you can grow your business.

Growing Your Business

As a small business owner, making the decision to grow your business is personal and difficult. Growing a business is a complicated and unique challenge. However, all larger companies started out as small businesses. This doesn't necessarily mean that expansion is always the right option or even possible to do. If your growth strategy is flawed or not properly managed then a growing business can turn out disastrous.

Some business owners choose to keep their operation small. If you have thought about growing your business, but are apprehensive, then you need to take a moment to objectively analyze what it would require for your business to grow. If your existing resources present you with limited natural growth, then you have only a few options to consider: buying another similar company, merging or forming an alliance with another company or developing something new.

None of these options are easier than another; they also aren't straightforward. Each option presents its own risks and rewards. Taking on this challenge will require a thorough analysis and evaluation of the competition and your own capabilities. After this analysis, you need to plan for your business growth in a way that exactly defines what growth means for your business. Depending on the route you choose to take, you may have to give up some control of your business.

RESEARCH THE MARKETS

It is important to take the time to analyze your existing market and any potential new markets before you put money into making a growth plan. This will help you to see what emerging trends are and how they will impact the future of the marketplace. You can also use this information to see if you can find new products.

A good place to go for information on the shifting market is the Internet and social media. You can also use it to find a niche that may not be entirely satisfied. If needed you can make some small changes to bring more business to you before fully committing to growing your business.

However, avoid the tendency to over analyze every detail and take no action. The goal is to use all the information you have and then make the decision that is best for you based on what you have.

CONSIDER INTERNAL GROWTH

Once you've reached your maximum capacity for delivering your existing products, you may need to hire additional employees in order to grow. If you are the sole proprietor, this can require major changes to the way you operate your business. Having employees also adds new issues when it comes to government mandates that influence the day to day operations of your business.

Before you start the search for a permanent employee, consider first using contract labor from a temporary agency. This allows you to see how having additional employees can benefit your business without the need to have the full responsibility of employees. Make sure you choose a person who is trained for the specific role you've planned, but they'll still often require on-the-job training for specific tasks. In your operating plan, you'll need to provide the cost of workspace, equipment, and supplies.

It is important to remember that internal growth and expansion of your existing customer base is going to take up a significant portion of your time and energy. This means some existing customers will likely see a decrease in personal contact and attention. Make sure they don't feel neglected. Dividing this time and energy can present a challenge, but you need to focus on it.

CONSIDER THE HUMAN FACTOR

The growth and complexity of you plan will determine how much additional resources you will need. You need to make this assessment as early on in the potential growth process as possible. If you need to hire additional people, this is something that will take time and effort.

As a small business, adding additional people is going to be a major event. This is because you don't have the option of getting an individual who is the perfect fit. Rather you want to get someone quickly and efficiently so they can immediate help your bottom line. You can't work as a large business and move people around or retrain them until you find something that meets their skills and potential.

You if are going to produce an entirely new product then you need to invest in both people and equipment. If you don't have what you need to find the right resources, then you may need to find someone to help. It is important to keep an eye on your current business and make sure it continues to thrive while growing into a new business. If you are taking up the majority of your time with growth, then things are going to start falling through the cracks, and your loyal customers will notice.

Whatever you choose to do should complement the culture and goals of your company. This is no more important than when thinking about an acquisition or merger. The combination needs to be seamless from both a personal and business perspective. The talents and capabilities of the businesses in both who they are and what they need to do should be compatible.

DETERMINING RISK

When growing your business, you need to make sure you don't let your emotion cloud your judgment. You need to have an objective assessment of what you're getting into. You may even want to get an outside opinion or two about the plans for your business. It is important to discuss it with people you trust and those who have the right experience to advise you. It doesn't mean you have to take the advice of others, but you should at least listen.

When you want to grow your business, develop a step-by-step plan but don't think you have to follow it specifically. If you find something impractical or better along the way, you should be able to change your plan and implement other things successfully. Be open to any change that can maximize the future of your business. Small businesses expand all the time, but most don't make it because they take on more than they can handle. Just proceed carefully and be objective, then you can successfully grow your business.

Now that you know what goes into making liquid soaps and growing your business into a success you can head out and start experimenting.

Final Words

Let's recap. First, you master the art of soap making, see if you enjoy creating various types and varieties on your own. Once you see that this is something you would want to start a business with, start small right from home. Make just a few varieties, package and label them properly. Your first try should be with social media like Facebook and such, see what kind of response you get. Once you get a few people to try out, ask them to post comments.

Once you have some buzz around your creation, next, you can take it to a few local craft and beauty supply stores around town and ask them if you can set up a display to showcase your products. Make sure to offer them good discounts/incentives so it can be a money-making opportunity for the store owners as well.

Next, you can try your product out in various local flea markets, set up a booth, and see what kind of response you get. After flea market, you would want to contact a few trade shows and see if you can get setup in one of the local or regional beauty product trade shows.

This is where you really want to be, as this is the venue where big companies can notice you and your products and if they like what you do, they can place a large order with you. So be prepared for it. It may take a couple of tries at various trade shows before you get noticed by a decent size company, so don't get discouraged easily.

Here are few trade organizations, gathering, and conferences related to soap and beauty products that you may want to become a member of and try to attend a few of these events every year.

https://www.fromnaturewithlove.com/tradeshows.asp

http://www.modernsoapmaking.com/freebies/soapmaking-gatherings-conferences-organizations/

https://www.soapguild.org/conference/

http://soapmakingbusiness.com/health-and-beauty-trade-shows

Last but not the least, I want to say THANK YOU for reading my book, this is my first try at writing, and it wouldn't have been possible without the help of my daughter Jennifer, who put her heart and soul into making sure this book comes together.

Since this was my first try at writing, I am sure I have made a few mistakes along the way, so I want to ask for your forgiveness ahead of time. And if you find it in your heart that I have tried my best to add some value to your passion than I would love to see a review of this book from you, it will sure put a big smile on my face. Once gain thank you so much!

One last advice I want to offer, at age 56, I can say this to man and women of all ages that if you have a dream to start a business and follow your passion, by all means, do it, make it come true, we all have this one tiny life to live, so let's make the best of it.

I am glad I followed my passion and was fortunate enough to see some real success, but till you try you will never know what awaits you out there. So give it a try, and if you stay sincere and work hard, you will see success. I guarantee it.

Good luck and God bless!

Appendix

Sample Corporate Articles

STATE OF ARKANSAS:

COUNTY OF PULASKI:

ARTICLES OF ORGANIZATION

OF

Natural Beauty and Soap Company LLC

The undersigned, acting as organizers of the Natural Beauty and Soap Company LLC under the Arkansas Limited Liability Company Act, adopt the following Articles of Organization for said Limited Liability Company.

Article I

Name of the Company

The name of the limited liability company is Natural Beauty and Soap Company LLC (the "Company").

Article II
Period of Duration

The period of duration is ninety (90) years from the date of filing of these Articles of Organization with the Arkansas Secretary of State, unless the Company is sooner dissolved.

Article III
Purpose of the Company

The Company is organized to engage in all legal and lawful purpose of producring and selling various beauty products.

Article IV
Registered Office and Agent

The Company's registered office is at address is 123 Main Court, Little Rock, Arkansas 12345; and the name and the address of the Company's initial registered agent is John Doe, 123 Main Court, Little Rock, Arkansas 12345.

Article V

Members of the Organization

There is one (1) member, all of which are identified in the Exhibit A attached hereto and a part hereof. The initial capital contribution agreed to be made by both members are also listed on Exhibit A. The members have not agreed to make any additional contributions, but may agree to do so in the future upon the terms and conditions as set forth in the Operating Agreement.

Article VI
Additional Members

The members, as identified in the Company's Operating Agreement, reserve the right to admit additional members and determine the Capital Contributions of such Members. Notwithstanding the foregoing, the additional Members may not become managing unless and until selected to such position as provided in Article VII of the Company's Operating Agreement.

Article VII
Contribution upon Withdrawal of Members

The members shall have the right to continue the company upon the death, retirement, resignation, expulsion, bankruptcy or dissolution of a member or occurrence of any event which terminates the continued membership of a member in the Company (collectively, "Withdrawal"), as long as there is at least One remaining member, and the remaining member agree to continue the Company by unanimous written consent within 90 days after the Withdrawal of a Member, as set forth in the Operating Agreement of the Company.

Article VIII

Manager

The name and business address of the initial manager is:

John Doe

Natural Beauty and Soap Company LLC
123 Main Court, Little Rock,
Arkansas 12345

The manager may be removed and replaced by the Members as provided in the Operating Agreement.

IN WITNESS WHEREOF, the undersigned have caused these Articles of Organization to be executed this .... Day of 2015

_____
_____ Natural Beauty and Soap
Company LLC   DATE

AN ARKANSAS CORPORATION

BY: John Doe

ITS: Managing Member

This instrument prepared by:

Jane Doe
999 Super Ct
Little Rock, AR 12345

EXHIBIT A

MEMBERS INTEREST	INTIAL CONTRIBUTION
John Doe 100%	Future Services Rendered

Made in United States
Troutdale, OR
11/20/2023

14755955R00156